JOHN JENKS

YES
SHE CAN

Biblical and Practical Reflections
on Women in Leadership
in the Church

D1637405

YES SHE CAN: Biblical and Practical Reflections on Women in Leadership in the Church

Copyright @2022 by John Jenks

Cover Design by Maria Connor

Proofreading and Formatting by Maria Connor, My Author Concierge

CONTENTS

ABOUT THE BOOK

Does the Bible teach us that women should be restricted from some areas of service and leadership in the church because of their gender OR does the Bible teach us women are called and gifted by God to serve and lead in the same way as men, without any restriction based on gender?

This is a question of vital importance. How one answers this question will have profound implications for individuals, the church, and the world the church serves. Wherever you might be in your own spiritual journey, your connection with the church, and your life experience around this question, *Yes She Can* will challenge and inspire you. This book offers an opportunity to:

- Gain clarity and move past some common misconceptions people have about this issue.
- Think carefully about how to interpret the Bible.

- Walk through portions of Scripture that are especially relevant to the question at hand.
- Be inspired by the beauty and hope found in the person of Jesus and his gospel.
- Wrestle with some of the essential and practical realities that surround this question.

You may have never read a book on this topic or perhaps you have studied this in great detail. Whatever your background, *Yes She Can* offers an excellent overview that will help you take a solid look at the question of women in leadership in the church. This book can assist people and churches in moving past the pain, fear, and confusion that often surround this issue. It is written and offered with the hope of leading people into a place of humble confidence and gracious conviction as they see God's vision for how people in the church can share life and ministry together.

———————

JOHN JENKS (M.DIV-Fuller Seminary) has served as a pastor with the Evangelical Covenant Church for more than thirty years.

WORDS OF SUPPORT

John Jenks has produced a treatment of the women and ministry issue that combines solid biblical reflection, thoughtful social reflection, and pastoral sensitivity. I recommend this without reservation and with enthusiasm.

—Dave Nystrom, Professor of Biblical Studies, Western Seminary

Oh yes, he did! John Jenks has written a clear and compelling book. *Yes She Can* pulls the issue of women in leadership out of the stuck places and frames the conversation in a way that everyone can access. His esteem of the Scriptures is clear, as is his ability to outline and explain the issues in luminous and helpful ways. This is an easy one to recommend.

—Dr. R. Scott Lisea, Campus Pastor, Westmont College

John Jenks has gifted pastors, church boards, and people in the pew with an invaluable resource for the glory of God and for the advancing of His Kingdom! For too long, churches have been deprived of the gifting entrusted to women. Thankfully, more and more churches are realizing the tragic loss of this reality and are enabling women who are called and gifted to serve in those gifts. *Yes She Can* is accessible, easy to read and understand, thorough, biblically sound, and inspiring. I literally could not stop reading it and encourage pastors, church boards, and congregants to give this book a thought-filled and prayerful read. You won't regret doing so!

—Pastor Gary Gaddini, Director of Unify, Transforming the Bay with Christ

John Jenks has managed to write a succinct yet thorough, humble yet confident book on women in ministry. Jenks has managed to bring a fresh wind to these discussions, dealing with real world questions that the reader has surely wondered about before. This is essential reading for all Christians.

—Shane Blackshear, Host of Seminary Dropout Podcast

John's years of humbly practicing mutuality and care for his sisters have allowed this beautiful book to make its way to us all; a book full of history, biblical imagery, reflection, and personal story that will invite you into a deeper journey and consideration. Whether you find yourself confused, concerned, convicted, or committed to women in ministry, you will be sure to benefit from the impressive research and wisdom in *Yes She Can*.

—**Meghan Safstrom Fisher, InterVarsity Christian Fellowship Staff Minister, Twin Ports MN/WI**

Anyone who wants to grapple seriously, biblically, and charitably with the egalitarian versus complementarian discussion should read this book. With a thoughtful understanding of the biblical texts and the passionate heart of a pastor, John Jenks challenges us to look at the question of women in leadership in the church at a deeper level. This book is an excellent resource for church pastors, leadership teams, and anyone who wants to engage in healthy conversation with others on this issue.

—**David McCowan, Lead Pastor, Community Covenant Church, Lenexa, KS**

Don't let the size of this book fool you. John packs an abundance of information from both Scripture and culture into its relatively few pages. The role of women in the church has been a much-debated topic for many years and a great number of books have been written on this subject. John's book stands with the best of them. He gives the reader a helpful and informative guide to what the Bible has to say regarding the use of one's gifts in the church, whether male or female. We truly hope that, because of this book, more churches, when asked if a woman can use her God-given gifts in a non-restrictive way, will answer, *Yes She Can!*

—**Ken and Mari Harrower, Mount Hermon Association, Inc./Camp and Conference Center, Mount Hermon, CA**

To Ann Jenks
You are the best.

A WORD OF THANKS FROM JOHN JENKS

I have been profoundly blessed to share life, faith, and ministry with wonderful people in these settings and places. God has touched my life through you. So, thanks to the people of:

Newport Covenant Church
Bellevue, WA
Cascade Covenant Church
North Bend, WA
Edgewater Covenant Church
Pittsburg, CA
Mount Hermon Christian Camp & Conference Center
Mount Hermon, CA
Lakeview Covenant Church
Duluth, MN
Samarkand Covenant Living Community
Santa Barbara, CA

FOREWORD

I have known **about** John Jenks most of my life, having grown up in the same church in California. However, I did not get to **know** John until he invited me to be a reader on this project; a book I am excited to get into the hands of men and women who will be encouraged and challenged by what they read.

I have served as a superintendent of churches for eleven years, and during that time I have experienced both the disappointment of churches that remain closed to the gifts of women, and the joy of encouraging and mentoring women to explore and persevere as they follow God's call into pastoral ministry. Our denomination has made significant progress toward a kingdom vision in which women and men work together in shared leadership based on gifts and call; a value that is grounded in our strong commitment to the centrality of the Word of God. However, like most evangelical denominations that affirm women in ministry, we have work to do to fully live out what we affirm. *Yes She Can* is an important resource that can shed light on why it is crucial we live into God's design for women and men.

I am grateful for this book and feel strongly that it will help those who are honestly exploring the path that leads to embracing the full inclusion of women in all leadership positions within the church. If you have reservations about women in ministry, I think this book is for you. John's pastoral heart permeates the tone and spirit of his work, making it accessible to anyone. I pray you will read it with an open mind and heart, inviting the Holy Spirit to be your guide, and may God lead you into the truth that transforms.

To God be the Glory in and through his church!

—Reverend Tammy Swanson-Draheim, President of the Evangelical Covenant Church

PREFACE

I am a grateful and passionate follower of Jesus Christ. I have served the church as a pastor for more than thirty years. I believe in the mission of the church as people coming together to experience and share the gospel of Jesus Christ. People matter: How we both view and treat each other inside and outside the church is of supreme importance. Further, the way we serve with the gifts the Holy Spirit gives us has immense significance for those serving and being served, and for the mission of Jesus.

As I follow Jesus, I strive to engage in a prayerful, thoughtful, humble, and open-minded exploration of the Bible. For many years, I've viewed the Bible as the Word of God and have tried to shape my life and ministry around the beautiful truth and wisdom of the Scriptures. I want to hear the Bible's message accurately. By that, I mean I want to avoid imposing my preferences on my interpretation, which might lead me to read into Scripture what I want it to say rather than hearing what it actually says. Is this challenging? Oh, yes. Good Bible study is hard work. I am committed to:

- Jesus Christ
- The Bible
- People
- The Church
- The Gospel and Mission of Jesus Christ

So, I've established where I am coming from as we start to consider this important question.

Does the Bible teach us that women should be restricted from some areas of service and leadership in the church because of their gender
OR
does the Bible teach us women are called and gifted by God to serve and lead in the same way as men, without any restriction based on gender?

This is the central question I'm raising in this book. It is what has motivated me to delve into questions critical to the church today and tomorrow. Are women called to serve in the church by following men from behind, or are women and men called into mission together, serving God side by side? Put another way, does God want a hierarchy of power and authority in the church determined by gender with men leading and women following?

As you and others read, I hope and pray we will become more closely aligned with the life God desires for us. As this happens, may we be changed by God's grace and truth, may

God's church be strengthened, and may this broken world that God loves experience a bit more of his healing grace.

May God bless you as you read!

John Jenks

Pastor, The Evangelical Covenant Church

2022

1

A FRAMEWORK FOR ENGAGING
THIS ISSUE

I've identified two different ways people have come to view the way women can or can't serve in the church. Pastors and biblical scholars have used a variety of terms to describe these positions and create a framework for engaging this issue. In this book, I primarily use "restrictive" and "nonrestrictive" to describe the ways we can think about the question at hand.

Restrictive

This perspective leads to a practice of limiting women in various ways from leading and/or teaching in the church. Where this line of restriction is drawn can vary dramatically among individual churches as well as larger denominations, but the common idea is this: Women need to be limited from leadership because of their gender.

What might this look like in practical terms? Here are some possible examples: Women cannot teach or preach, women cannot be pastors, women can be youth or associate pastors but not lead pastors, women cannot serve on a church's staff or on a church's primary leadership group. Sometimes the restrictions are qualified. For example, women cannot lead a Bible study or ministry team if men are part of that group/team, women can teach or lead in some settings or on some days but not in other settings or on other days, and so on.

This line of restriction can be found in all kinds of places, but the larger point is the existence of a line of restriction for women that does not apply to men.

This "restrictive" perspective is sometimes described as "complementarian." This term applies to the belief that men and women are called to different and complementary roles for which they are best suited within marriage and/or church life. For example, only men are the head of the home, thus they have greater authority in the home, and its companion belief that only men can be pastors and primary church teachers and leaders.

The complementarian belief holds that women are created to live with a "role" or "position" of being in submission to the authority of men. Women are said to have equal value to men while also having different God-given roles within a hierarchy of male leadership and authority.

Non-Restrictive

This perspective promotes the view that men and women are free to serve in the church based on their character, faith, calling, and gifts without limitations based on gender. This position is sometimes described as "egalitarian" or "biblical equality." Some prefer the terms "mutuality" or "interdependent" to describe this position.

Among evangelical Christians, "non-restrictive" refers to the idea that the Bible affirms a genuine equality and shared calling among men and women. So, men and women, while different in complementary ways, are invited by God into equal opportunities for leadership and service within marriage and/or church life. Marriage is viewed as an equal partnership and women can serve in any area of church life and leadership.

Non-Restrictive/Egalitarian doesn't mean identical

This approach doesn't imply that male and female are the same. An egalitarian perspective affirms gender differences as real, mysterious, and important. I've never met an "egalitarian" Christian who did not affirm male and female as both different and complementary.

However, biblical egalitarianism rejects the belief that the Bible teaches women are to live in a "role" or "position" subordinate to men. In this biblical egalitarianism, female subordination is not God's best and intended vision for humanity. Rather, men and women were created to live in unity and oneness as individuals created in the image of God. In this view, women and men share a very real equality of worth, rank, privilege, and standing. In its essence, this means women and men are both created in God's image and called to serve God together, and both are offered the gift of salvation and given gifts for ministry. No calling exists for women to live within a hierarchy of male authority as an essential part of one's core identity.

In practice, this means women are viewed and treated through a lens of biblical equality that invites them to serve in every area of the church. This understanding goes beyond questions of equality or justice and into God's vision for unity and community among both men and women.

I realize there are variations of these views, and no term is perfect to describe either the "complementarian" perspective or the "egalitarian" perspective. I'm using the terms *restrictive* and *non-restrictive* to help us focus on the essence of each position and the practical realities and results coming from them.

What I Believe

I advocate for the position that women are called and gifted by God to serve in all areas of the church. No restrictions on their service and leadership based on gender should exist. I come to this position because I believe this is the message of Jesus, the message of the Bible, and the message of what the Bible calls "The Gospel" (The Good News).

So, restrictive or non-restrictive? What does the Bible say to us as we strive to share life and ministry together in the church? What are the consequences that flow from how we understand this important issue?

SIX PRELIMINARY NOTES TO START

As we begin, I want to offer six notes that can help us approach this subject with transparency and objectivity. There are several myths and misunderstandings that can lead to confusion without some initial clarification. Please keep these in mind as we move forward.

This is an issue of biblical interpretation—not biblical inspiration or authority.

This is a critical observation: Many prayerful, intelligent, and sincere followers of Jesus have studied the Scriptures and come to different conclusions on a given subject or on the meaning of a specific portion of Scripture. When it comes to interpreting what the Bible has to say about women in leadership in the church, this is certainly true. Many wise and devoted people have an authentic faith in Christ and honor the Bible as God's Word, but don't share my perspective on this issue. Their conclusion or mine has nothing to do with who has greater conviction about their belief in Jesus or in the authority of Scripture.

Some say that those who believe the Bible teaches that women are called and gifted to serve with no restrictions based on their gender must, therefore, not believe in the authority of Scripture itself. These individuals try to turn this into a question of greater conviction. Who really believes in the authority and integrity of the Bible? This is inaccurate, unfair, and confuses the issue. Put simply, it is a mistake to say that holding the non-restrictive position of biblical equality reflects a soft or low view of Scripture.

I've heard the argument stated this way: If you believe the Bible teaches that women can lead and serve in the church without restrictions, you just don't believe in the authority of the Bible itself. This delivers an unfortunate message, the essence of which is: If you don't interpret the Bible like I do, I will just accuse you of not believing in the inspiration and authority of the Bible. This kind of simplistic accusation distorts the conversation in a disrespectful and manipulative way. Instead, let's change the perspective and tone and say: We both agree the Bible is the Word of God, but we have different interpretations about what it teaches us about women in leadership in the church.

For many years, pastor and author John Armstrong embraced a perspective that restricted women from leading in the church. Then, as he continued to study the Bible, God changed his perspective. In his journey, he shares how important it is to recognize this is an issue of biblical interpretation – not biblical authority. Armstrong offers this powerful statement in Chapter One of *How I Changed My Mind about*

Women in Leadership: Compelling Stories from Prominent Evangelicals:

My vision now can be rather simply stated. I long to see all Christian men wholeheartedly giving up on their own agendas and following Christ in humble, complete collaboration with their Christian sisters. And I long to see my Christian sisters follow Christ in precisely the same way. Our goal, as both male and female, is not to compete or to struggle with each other over gender roles. Our goal is to advance the kingdom of Christ as fellow heirs of the grace of God. For me this is so basic that I wonder why it took me so long to see it.

The contributors to this book all embrace the authority of God's Word over their lives. We are earnest about obeying God. We are seeking to do serious biblical exegesis and to apply the implications of the gospel to our time. This is why we cannot keep silent about changing our minds about women in Christian ministry. This is not about winning debates but about obeying Christ and being faithful members of his church.

Where does this perspective of "biblical equality" come from?

As a follower of Jesus, I want to view all of life through the lens of the gospel of Jesus Christ and biblical revelation. I join with many others who, throughout church history, have advocated for what we might call "biblical equality" because they see it in Scripture and believe it is in harmony with the gospel of Jesus Christ. Here are two examples.

The changes affecting women in the modern era have obviously influenced the church's thinking, but the ministry of women is neither derived from society's ideas nor a partner to its extremes. For a tradition that is based on "Where is it written?" only one foundation is satisfactory for having women minister in the name of Jesus Christ. Women ought to minister not because society says so but because the Bible leads the church to such a conclusion. (Evangelical Covenant Church. "The Biblical & Theological Basis for Women in Ministry," https://covchurch.org/wp-content/uploads/sites/2/2011/02/2-Women-in-Ministry.pdf)

We hold to this conviction of co-leadership and gender equity not because of popular culture or political correctness, but because of how we read the Scriptures together. — John Wenrich, Pastor / Former President of the Evangelical Covenant Church (Peters, Marianne. "Called by God," *Covenant Companion Magazine;* September 2019)

In a healthy, biblically functioning community, men and women are called and gifted to serve side by side without a hierarchy of male authority and power. This position is not based on any form of modern feminism or driven by current cultural winds. This position is rooted in a discerned understanding of what the Bible teaches.

While this book focuses on the question of women serving in the church with or without restrictions, the question of what the Bible teaches about marriage and the roles of husband and wife is also important.

The Bible does speak to the responsibilities of both husband and wife. While I don't focus on this, I believe the Bible shares a beautiful vision for marriage when a man and a woman come together as husband and wife in a spirit of love, unity, service, and mutual submission. I believe interpretations of New Testament passages that conclude the husband should always have a position of authority over the wife while emphasizing the wife's submission to her husband are inaccurate and problematic. Much could be said on this, but I contend the calling to mutual submission in Ephesians 5:21 offers a beautiful framework for marriage. There are many helpful resources that explore the biblical teaching on marriage. Among them I would recommend Lucy Peppiatt's book, *Rediscovering Scripture's Vision for Women: Fresh Perspectives on Disputed Texts.*

How one understands the issue of women serving and leading in the church does not automatically lead to specific positions on other issues, such as human sexuality.

Some will say if a church or individual accepts women into leadership this will automatically mean they'll become supportive of same-sex marriage. This is simplistic and inaccurate. This creates confusion and doesn't allow for a healthy conversation on the specific question of women in leadership in the church. Human sexuality is a broad and important subject that needs to be engaged in with great care. However, it is a mistake to say that if a church or person accepts women as leaders in the church this automatically means they will hold or develop a certain view of human sexuality or a specific position on other issues.

The issue addressed in this book is important.

Among the many reasons this issue is important is its influence on how people are viewed and treated. The position and practices a church develops on women in leadership in the church will profoundly affect its ministry, outreach, pastoral care, and discipleship. It will influence the degree to which people are able to live fully into the calling God has entrusted them with. How women are either limited from serving or free to serve will make a difference in the lives of both men and women. Men and women are different, and churches need what both men and women can bring to the life and leadership of the church.

This is also a crucial issue because it reflects our understanding of the full power and message of the gospel of Jesus Christ. Tammy Swanson-Draheim is a pastor and currently serves as president of the Evangelical Covenant Church. I appreciate her words from the September 2019 article "Called by God" in *Covenant Companion Magazine*:

You will hear occasionally people say this is not essential, or they will put it in the category of a 'woman's' issue. It's a gospel issue —the gospel of Jesus Christ. When we relegate it to some category of nonessential, then people can treat it in an entirely different manner. Are we teaching the complete gospel? Do we believe that what Jesus did on the cross was sufficient to restore broken humanity? Because when we decide that women don't have the ability to fully live into their call, we're literally saying that Jesus's work on the cross wasn't sufficient. We can choose to live in the shadow of the fall—or the light of the resurrection.

While I value the terms "biblical equality" and "egalitarian," I think they can sometimes lead to a limited understanding of what is at stake. They can cause some people to assume this is only about "justice." It is indeed an important justice issue but it's so much more. When it comes to either restricting women from using their gifts or freeing them to serve in all areas of the church, we are engaged in multiple intersecting issues. This is a:

Gospel issue: Will we embrace the biblical vision for how the gospel transforms our vision for people, relationships, and community life? Will we live into the beautiful implications and opportunities the gospel proclaims as it leads us to remove so many of the social barriers and forms of discrimination that have plagued the human family?

Mission issue: Will we create a culture of freedom in our churches that allows men and women to serve together and complement each other in all areas of the church life and leadership? Will we see how inviting women to lead and serve in all areas of our church life can enhance our discipleship, pastoral care, outreach, and overall ministry impact?

Power issue: Will the church live in and display a use of power that is kingdom driven and reflective of the message of Jesus?

Community issue: Will we share life and ministry together in the church where women and men live in the freedom of genuine appreciation and respect for each other? Will we remove the way women are marginalized when they are restricted from serving and leading because of their gender?

Identity issue: Will we affirm that being made in God's image is central to our identity? Believing women and men are both made in the image of God and are also different from each other as female and male, will we position ourselves to reflect God's image as both male and female throughout our church?

Indeed, this is not just a "woman's" concern or only a matter of "justice." It is a vital question for individuals and churches, and it will shape their thoughts, values, actions, and relationships. This is a crucial concern for every church because it impacts individuals and influences ministry on multiple levels.

What if this "non-restrictive" perspective of "biblical equality" is new to you or difficult for you?

I understand that for some people this perspective can challenge one of their most cherished beliefs. It may run counter to what a spiritual mentor or pastor has taught you. If this describes you, please know I appreciate how hard it can be to consider a different viewpoint. You may read all of my thoughts here and never share my position, but I hope you will still benefit from the experience. I invite you to read on with an open mind.

3

INTERPRETING AND UNDERSTANDING THE BIBLE

Before we begin walking through portions of the biblical message, it's helpful to think about how we can position ourselves to interpret the Bible accurately. Here are a few principles of biblical interpretation I have found helpful.

Be honest, self-aware, humble, and open.

We all come to the Scriptures with our own story. No one is completely objective. All of us have been influenced along the way and have developed a "filter" or "lens" from which we view life and process information and ideas. This doesn't mean we can't think well, pursue objectivity, or gain clarity. It does mean we do well to be honest and self-aware about what has shaped our assumptions regarding any given issue, including women in leadership in the church.

As we come to the question of what the Bible teaches us, everyone can benefit from pausing and offering this prayer:

"God, help me to see what the Scriptures are saying, even if it might stretch or surprise me."

Read with tradition but not through tradition.

It helps to pay attention to our personal faith tradition and cultural context because they influence how we hear and initially respond to any perspective we encounter. We can learn a lot from when and where the church has given instruction on any given issue. However, we can also affirm that:

- The Bible is our guide and the source of God's revelation and truth. As it points us to the authority of Jesus himself and his gospel, the Bible is a higher authority than any church tradition.
- The church has been wrong and had blind spots, even for long periods of time.
- There have been times when the church has changed its positions and practices and these changes have been valuable and brought our life into closer alignment with biblical wisdom.

We can value our cultural and faith tradition, but we need to avoid reading the Bible through that tradition in a way that causes us to miss what the Bible is really saying. We need to not conclude the Bible is saying something because that is what we want it to say.

Sometimes our personal cultural context will shape our assumptions and conclusions more than we realize. For example, it is worth considering how each of the following factors may influence how you interpret the Bible.

- Being an American, or Russian, or Brazilian, or African or Asian, and so on.
- Living in the 21st or 17th or 6th century.
- Living as a rich person or poor person.
- Living as a person of a specific ethnicity.
- Living as a person who has embraced a certain political philosophy.

So let's pay attention to our own story, context, and tradition as we read the Scriptures, but let's not force the Scriptures to conform to our personal story and cultural values.

Let's also remember sometimes we are wise to change our minds. The early church models this for us in Acts 15. As these individuals wrestled with their tradition, they struggled and then ultimately changed as they affirmed a new position that led them to embrace the full inclusion of the Gentiles in the church. Reading Scripture with our tradition in mind but not through our tradition in a rigid way was important in God's movement in the church reformation in the 1500s.

Think about exegesis, hermeneutics, and context.

Exegesis is the task of discovering what a given portion of Scripture meant to the original audience. *Hermeneutics* involves understanding what a given text is saying to us today, paying attention to the original intent and meaning and then seeking to apply that meaning appropriately today. When we do both well, we're on the path toward accurately understanding the Bible and appropriately applying biblical truth in our lives.

Giving careful attention to the historical and cultural context of any given portion of the Bible is valuable, as is recognizing the type of literature we're reading. Different books of the Bible reflect different "genres" of literature. When reading a story, letter, or message written thousands of years ago in a different language and in a cultural setting very different from our own, we do well to pay close attention to context and the way language and communication work.

In Chapter 13 of the book *Discovering Biblical Equality: Complementarity without Hierarchy*, Peter Davids says this about the dynamics of language and communication:

Language is an expression of a given culture existing in space and time. It takes its meaning from the definitions that culture gives to certain sounds and their associated graphic symbols. It is a truism that any given word, or its associated sound, in one culture may have a different meaning from the same word or sound in another. Furthermore, words in all languages change their meanings over time.

Let Scripture help us interpret Scripture.

Every portion of Scripture is both valuable and connected. When looking at any specific verse or section of the Bible, it's important to pay attention to what other portions of Scripture might say on the same subject. If there is a passage that is especially complex and difficult to understand, it can be helpful to draw from other portions of Scripture that speak to a given topic with greater clarity. Consider these words from Stephen G. Dempster in *Manifesto for Theological Interpretation*:

There are many words of God within the canon and seeing them as a whole helps us to see various accents and elements in all their diversity as well as their unity. The larger canonical context is able to show how the various parts of the canon connect, interrelate, reveal the major accents and emphases, and dialogue with one another. Thus, the canon is not flat and one-dimensional but has depth, contour, and texture and must be understood in its rich and multifaceted totality.... The exodus event is viewed as more important than Paul's request for Timothy to come and bring his coat (II Timothy 4:13). ... The command to circumcise in Genesis is viewed in light of the command not to circumcise in Galatians.

Remember the big when interpreting the small.

As we look to Scripture to help us interpret Scripture, we must pay attention to the larger themes of biblical revelation and stay alert to the progress of revelation. What is revealed to Abraham, Moses, and others is not the final word. We benefit from seeing the trajectory of God's revelation, movement in history, and the redemptive work in Christ. There is a progression of revelation over the course of history and in the flow of the biblical story.

This principle helps us avoid the problematic approach of isolating any small portion of Scripture or an individual verse and building a massive position from it while minimizing or ignoring other passages that speak to the same issue. As we look at any individual verse or passage of Scripture, we need to remember the preponderance of biblical teaching on any given topic, the big message of God's redemptive work in history, and the central message of the gospel of Jesus Christ.

We do well to integrate and understand each verse within the larger section it is part of, the original book it is in, and within the Bible as a whole. When we do this, we avoid "proof texting" our way to a position, where we focus on one or two texts but don't do the important work of seeing what the whole Bible is saying.

We need to remember that everything is not of equal importance. There are central issues and aspects of the Christian faith and there are peripheral ones. We see Jesus recognizing this in some of his conflicts with the Pharisees over the Sabbath laws (Luke 6:1-11). We also see this when Jesus talked about the emphasis on tithing while neglecting what he called "the more important matters" (Matthew 23:23).

Here is one example of the danger of selective literal interpretation and what happens if we isolate a verse and don't attempt to understand it in context. Consider these statements from the book of Ecclesiastes in the Old Testament:

I have seen all things that are done under the sun; all of them are meaningless, a chasing after the wind. (1:14)

So I came to hate life because everything done here under the sun is so troubling. Everything is meaningless —(2:17)

If we isolate these verses and interpret them literally, some might conclude the Bible teaches us there is no purpose or meaning in life. These verses need to be understood in context and within the larger message of the Bible. The Bible teaches us in powerful ways that there is indeed real purpose in life for everyone. But if we isolate these two verses while ignoring the larger context of the book of Ecclesiastes and the whole of Scripture, confusion and misunderstandings easily result.

Unfortunately, this often happens when some isolate a few verses that they think justify restricting women from church leadership. They fail to understand how the context of the verses inform their meaning, while also missing how the "big" message of the gospel and the Scriptures point us to a beautiful vision for women and men sharing ministry and leadership in the church.

As we think about the biblical message related to women in leadership in the church, we do well to keep the *BIG* message in mind. Consider these major biblical themes:

- Men and women are equally and fully created in the image of God and called to serve God together while ruling over God's creation. (Genesis 1-2)
- There are many examples in Scripture of women leading as they served God and supported his mission in the world. (Judges 4-5, Romans 16)
- The Holy Spirit is poured out on both men and women who are both called to spread the Word of God. (Acts 2)
- Spiritual gifts are clearly given to everyone with no mention of any limitations or restrictions based on gender. (I Corinthians 12, Romans 12, Ephesians 4)
- Unity in the Body of Christ where every person and gift are honored and valued as of great importance. (I Corinthians 12).
- There is a strong calling to love and respect one another in the Body of Christ. (John 13:34-35)

- We see a strong calling to humility and to beware of the dangers of power. (Philippians 2, Mark 10)
- It is compelling to see the revolutionary ways Jesus honored women and invited them into his ministry even as he navigated life in a highly patriarchal context. (John 4, Luke 7:44-48, Luke 8:1-3, Luke 10:38-42, Matthew 28:8-10)
- The gospel of Jesus Christ shows us the heart of God for all people regardless of nationality, race, class, or gender. (Galatians 3:28, Acts 15, Matthew 25 & 28, Acts 1, Philemon, Romans 1)
- The gospel itself and its implications are crucial. This informs our vision for people, how we treat people, and how we understand the reality of the new creation that is available in Christ. (II Corinthians 5, Ephesians 2)

Be careful not to turn a specific, temporary, and local word into a universal and timeless command or prohibition.

I have heard some people proudly declare that they read the Bible very literally and just take it for what it clearly says. They often do this when isolating a specific verse or passage and say something like this:

"It is so clear – how can you miss it – just read the Bible and don't confuse the obvious message with your hermeneutical maneuvering that avoids the plain and clear teaching of Scripture."

This approach often creates confusion by not recognizing how some portions of Scripture had a specific meaning for their original audience. These passages still have value for us today but may not be meant to be applied literally in a simplistic, universal, or timeless way. We need to learn how to distinguish between universal and timeless principles and local descriptions, instructions, and applications.

Some say that because everything Paul wrote addressed specific situations, we can't really distinguish between what is "timeless" and what is "temporary." However, this misses the point. To best understand and apply the Bible's message, we need to think about exegesis, hermeneutics, and context. There can be eternal truth even as we understand a biblical passage might have temporary dynamics and applications. As we recognize the specific temporary context, we have the best opportunity to accurately understand the meaning of a text and begin to discern how to best apply it today.

Think about it this way. Most followers of Jesus who value the Bible would agree that the following are timeless and universal biblical instructions:

- Love God
- Love your neighbor
- Care for the poor
- Love mercy and do justice
- Live with generosity and compassion
- Let the light of Jesus shine through you in a dark world
- Worship God with gratitude and joy
- Pray often
- Trust God when you face hardships

But not all portions of Scripture are best understood as time-less and universal instructions. Some scriptural instructions and descriptions are best understood as words with some measure of limited, specific, local, and temporary applica-tion. If we should "just read the Bible and interpret it literally and do what it clearly says," then how does that approach apply to these verses?

- Greet one another with a holy kiss. (I Corinthians 16:20)
- Wash each other's feet. (John 13)
- Sell everything you have and give to the poor. (Mark 10:21)
- Sell your possessions and share everything with others in the church. (Acts 2:42-45)
- If you lust, cut your eyes out. (Matthew 5:27-29)
- Women should not wear pearls or gold jewelry. (I Timothy 2:9)
- Drink some wine for your health. (I Timothy 5:23)
- Don't pray in public; when you pray, go to your room and pray in private. (Matthew 6:6)
- If you want to follow me (Jesus), you need to hate your parents. (Luke 14: 26)

How would you interpret and apply these verses if you focused on them apart from the larger message of Scripture and without considering their specific context? Most Chris-tian people I know understand these verses with an apprecia-tion for how the context helps us appropriately interpret them and avoid applying these verses in a literal, universal, or timeless way.

We need to be consistent in the way we interpret the Bible. I've never met a Christian person who applies all the verses above in a literal way or even contends we should.

I have had conversations with people who have quoted I Timothy 2:12 and said this verse clearly proves women should never be leaders in the church. However, when challenged a bit, sometimes they will realize and acknowledge they are not very consistent. They are choosing to selectively apply a method of interpretation to I Timothy 2:12 that they'd never use when interpreting the verses listed above. (More on I Timothy 2 later.) All Scripture is true, and all Scripture has eternal relevance. However, all Scripture is not designed to be applied universally in a literal way, especially when it is isolated and not considered in light of its own context and the full biblical message.

Expect some tension, uncertainty, and hard work.

The Bible is not always crystal clear or easy to understand. Even with the best Biblical scholarship, we're sometimes working with limited information. While I have a high level of conviction for my position on women in leadership in the church, I recognize there are complexities with some of the biblical texts. But it is always worth the work to keep coming back to God's Word with an open mind and a humble heart! May God's Spirit help us understand his wisdom and will as we come to his Word. I have found the quote below helpful in understanding the nature of Scripture and how we approach it.

From the introduction in Gordon D. Fee and Doug Stuart's book, *How to Read the Bible for All Its Worth*:

Because the Bible is God's Word, it has eternal relevance; it speaks to all mankind, in every age and in every culture. Because it is God's word, we must listen – and obey. But because God chose to speak his word through human words in history, every book in the Bible also has historical particularity; each document is conditioned by the language, time, and culture in which it was originally written (and in some cases also by the oral history it had before it was written down). Interpretation of the Bible is demanded by the "tension" that exists between eternal relevance and its historical particularity.

4

WALKING THROUGH THE SCRIPTURES

C onsider the following Scriptures and how they influence our understanding of men and women's service in the church.

GENESIS 1-3

How we understand the first three chapters of Genesis significantly influences our understanding of the core value, identity, and calling of both men and women. This passage informs our understanding of God's vision for people sharing life and mission together. We see a consistent expression of God's creative work in Genesis 1 (1:10, 1:12, 1:18, 1:21, 1:25).

- God spoke
- It happened – "It was so"
- God observed/saw his creation
- God's creation was identified as good

Then in Genesis 1:26-28 we read:

[26] Then God said, "Let us make mankind in our image, in our likeness, so that they may rule over the fish in the sea and the birds in the sky, over the livestock and all the wild animals, and over all the creatures that move along the ground."

[27] So God created mankind in his own image,

in the image of God he created them;

male and female he created them.

[28] God blessed them and said to them, "Be fruitful and increase in number; fill the earth and subdue it. Rule over the fish in the sea and the birds in the sky and over every living creature that moves on the ground."

We see here the incredible message that all people are made in the very image of God. It should be noted the word "mankind" here simply means humanity without giving priority or greater value to the male gender. As people made in the very image of God, we have a unique God-given identity with profound implications.

It's clear in this text that both men and women bear the image of God equally and fully. Women do not have a reduced measure of God's image. The image of God that men are created with is in no way superior to women. Men and women both have a shared identity and calling in their humanity as image bearers. Men and women also have a real distinction from each other in their masculinity and femininity.

Men and women each have something to share that needs to be received. If either male or female are restricted from sharing their voice, gifts, and presence in the church leadership and community, we are vulnerable to missing the opportunity to live fully into our identity as the church God wants us to be.

Women and men are also called together into mission. The Scripture says *they* are to rule over the earth. God said to men and women, with no mention of a gender-driven hierarchy or structure of authority, go and rule over the earth. Men and women equally and fully bear the image of God and are equally and fully called into mission together.

God says over and over his creation was good and then we hear this amazing observation in Genesis 1:31:

God saw all that he had made, and it was very good.

We see in Genesis not just the activity of God as our creator. We also begin to see a vision for his original and intended best for humanity. We are told not only that God created this world; we begin to understand why. We see a powerful and beautiful vision of God's desire for his good creation: Men and women united with God, living and serving together in unity, enjoying God's creation, reflecting the image of God, and ruling together over the world. In Genesis 2:18 we read:

The Lord God said, "It is not good for man to be alone. I will make a helper suitable for him."

God creates "woman" so men and women could share life and community together. The primary motivation here was to address what was not good – aloneness. God created men and women for each other so they could experience oneness, community, and mission.

There is no description of any need for or presence of a hierarchy of male authority. Some have understood this verse as a justification for believing God's original intent was for men to be in authority over women because the woman is referred to as a "helper." They try to use Genesis 1-3 to justify establishing a hierarchy of male leadership and authority in the home, church, and world. Several problems with this interpretation exist and often involve reading something into the text, perhaps based on our own tradition or preferences, which is just not there.

If we let this text speak for itself, there is no reason to assume a helper reflects a subordinate role or relationship. In fact, the Hebrew word "suitable" (*knegdo*) has a meaning of "equal to" or "corresponding to." Also, it is important to remember that the word used in Genesis 2:18 for "helper" (*ezer*) is used in several other places in the Old Testament, most often referring to God himself. The word offers the idea of someone who is strong coming alongside someone who needs help.

In *Two Views on Women in Ministry*, Linda Belleville says:

All of the other nineteen occurrences of "ezer" in the Old Testament have to do with the assistance that someone of strength offers to someone in need, namely, help from a God, king, an ally, or an army. Moreover, fifteen of the nineteen references speak of the help God alone can provide.

One example of this is in Psalm 33:20:

We wait in hope for the Lord; he is our help and our shield

With this word used most often in Scripture as a reference to God as our helper, it becomes problematic to assume a helper in Genesis 2 must refer to one assisting another from a lower position of authority or power.

Some have suggested that because Adam was created first this implies men are in some way superior to women or designed to be in a position of authority over women. This again involves reading something into the text that is not present. In the Genesis account of creation there is nothing that says the order of creation reflects a hierarchy of power based on gender. The Bible is simply describing the activity and sequence of an ordered and purposeful creation. One cannot legitimately argue humans are the apex of creation because they were created last and then argue men are a superior or higher form of creation because they were created first. Any effort to justify male authority based on the order of creation has significant biblical and logical problems.

In Genesis 1-3, we see at least four strong reasons to believe God's intended desire was for men and women to live and serve together without a hierarchy of male power and authority over women.

1. Men and women are clearly created equally and fully in the image of God and called equally and fully into mission. This is essential to their identity and humanity. God says they are to rule over creation together. God does not say men will

rule; he says men and women will rule together ... "they" being a key word in Genesis 1:27. God speaks to both men and women together as he blesses and calls them to rule over the earth together. In 1:28 we read: **"God blessed *them* and said to *them,* be fruitful and ..."**

2. The absence in Genesis 1-2 of any clear description of a hierarchy with men as leaders and women as followers is significant. Genesis 1-2 gives us a picture of God's intended desire for men and women to share community, life, and mission in a united way characterized by mutuality. We can find no statement in Genesis that implies men are designed to have dominion over women. On the contrary, Genesis does clearly say men and women are to share the calling to rule over the earth together.

3. Genesis 3 is telling. Following what many theologians call *The Fall*, by which sin and brokenness enter the world through the disobedience of Adam and Eve, we find a description of the painful consequences of their actions. Some refer to this as *The Curse*, describing the results of our rebellion against God that begins with Adam and Eve. In Genesis 3:16-19 we read:

[16] To the woman he said,

"I will make your pains in childbearing very severe;

> **with painful labor you will give birth to children.**

Your desire will be for your husband,

> **and he will rule over you."**

¹⁷ To Adam he said, "Because you listened to your wife and ate fruit from the tree about which I commanded you, 'You must not eat from it,'

Cursed is the ground because of you;

> **through painful toil you will eat food from it**
>
> **all the days of your life.**

¹⁸ It will produce thorns and thistles for you,

> **and you will eat the plants of the field.**

¹⁹ By the sweat of your brow

> **you will eat your food**

until you return to the ground,

> **since from it you were taken;**

for dust you are

> **and to dust you will return."**

We see here the entrance of a deep darkness into the human experience. Loss, hurt, brokenness, and death are now present. In this, we hear how man will now rule over woman, one gender having power over the other. In some traditions, people have interpreted this passage as a description of God's desire for humanity. Some have pointed to this text as a justification for men to have a position of power and authority over women. This is a tragic and misguided interpretation.

What is clear in this passage is this: Man's dominion over woman is part of the curse. Genesis 3 is not a prescription for what God wants; it is a description of what breaks God's heart. This chapter describes the reality and results of sin. *The Curse* is what Christ wants to free us from, not an ideal we should strive for. It is significant and sobering to see the Bible's clear description of a male hierarchy in Genesis 3 as something associated with the tragic result of sin.

I agree with Beth Allison Barr who says in Chapter One of *The Making of Biblical Womanhood: How the Subjugation of Women Became Gospel Truth:*

Instead of assuming that patriarchy is instituted by God, we must ask whether patriarchy is a product of sinful human hands. (And from Genesis 3)... And there it was – the Biblical explanation for the birth of patriarchy. The first human sin built the first human power hierarchy.

Some complementarians accept patriarchy as a valid term to describe their position, but most resist the use of that term. The definition of patriarchy in dictionary.com is "a social system in which power is held by men, through cultural norms and customs that favor men and withhold opportunities for women." I believe this is an accurate description of what the restrictive position promotes, and we can see this tragically emerging in Genesis 3:16-19.

Here are two helpful quotes. First, from Ruth Haley-Barton in Chapter 2 of *How I Changed My Mind about Women in Leadership: Compelling Stories from Prominent Evangelicals*:

Domination by one gender over the other was not God's ideal that we were supposed to work hard to uphold; rather, they were predictions of consequences that we were to work hard to over-

come and that Jesus himself would fully overcome as a part of our redemption.

When we require women to pay over and over again for Eve's transgression with her silence and submission, we negate the full redemptive power of the gospel. Rather than becoming an example of relationships, we model the curse. Rather than living out God's ideal (as seen in Genesis 1) so that our presence in society begins to transform it, we allow ourselves to be squeezed into the world's mold of sexism and discrimination.

Second, from the Willow Creek Church Leadership Seminar, Pastor John Ortberg said:

Because of the fall, the relationship between male and female, which was meant to be oneness, has become a power struggle and is now filled with pain. So, the world became a place of struggle for dominance. While we were made for community, power takes over when community breaks down.

4. Another important insight in Genesis 1-3 that supports the position that men and women were created to live in unity without a hierarchy of male authority is this: The Christian faith declares there is one God – who is eternally present in three persons – Father, Son, and Holy Spirit. One of the clues to the relational nature of God as trinity is seen in the reference to God using the plural language in Genesis 1:26 when it says:

Then God said, "Let *us* make mankind in *our* image, in *our* likeness ...

The word *trinity* is not in the Bible but for many centuries Christian people have affirmed this word as descriptive of the relational nature of God that we see in Scripture. As people made in the image of God, we reflect a God of relational oneness and community and have a calling to this kind of relational life with one another. God as Father, Son, and Holy Spirit exists without any internal hierarchy. Father, Son, and Holy Spirit live together with ongoing and eternal generosity, self-giving love, and community. Consider these Scriptures and a few quotes that speak to the amazing internal relational life of the trinity which people are created in the image of.

No one has ever seen God, but the one and only son, who is himself God and is in closest relationship with the Father. (John 1:18)

The Spirit glorifies Jesus. (John 16:14)

The Son glorifies the Father. (John 17:4)

The Father Glorifies the Son. (John 17:5)

The Father will give you another advocate to help you and be with you forever – The Spirit of truth ... You know him for he lives with you and will be in you ...I am in the Father and you are in me and I am in you. (John 14:16-17)

When the Advocate comes, whom I will send to you from the Father – the Spirit of truth who goes out from the father – he will testify about me. (John 15:26)

I came from the Father and entered the world; now I am leaving the world and going back to the Father. (John 16:27)

Another expression of the trinity in Scripture is found in Matthew 28:19 when Jesus instructs his followers to baptize new believers "in the name of the Father and of the Son and of the Holy Spirit." Consider these powerful reflections from Chapter 14 of Timothy Keller's book, *The Reason for God: Belief in an Age of Skepticism*, regarding the beauty, mystery and nature of God as Father, Son and Holy Spirit:

The inner life of the triune God, however, is utterly different. The life of the trinity is characterized not by self-centeredness but by mutual self-giving love. When we delight and serve someone else, we enter into a dynamic around him or her, we center on the interests and desires of the other. That creates a dance, particularly if there are three persons, each of whom moves around the other two. So it is, the Bible tells us.... Each person of the trinity loves, adores, defers to, and rejoices in the others. This creates a dynamic, pulsating dance of joy and love.

Also from Cornelius Plantinga in *Engaging God's World: A Christian Vision of Faith, Learning, and Living*:

The Father ... Son ... and Holy Spirit glorify each other .... At the center of the universe, self-giving love is the dynamic currency of the Trinitarian life of God. The persons within God exalt, commune with, and defer to one another. ... When the early Greek Christians spoke of perichoresis in God they meant that each divine person harbors the others at the center of his being. In constant movement of overture and acceptance each person envelops and encircles the others.

It is important to understand how being created in the very image of God gives us a vision for God's best intentions and desires for us. As children of God who bear his image, we were created with the unique capacity to live in union with God. We also were created for a relational life with each other that is reflective of the relational life within God himself. Jesus refers to this in his prayer for his followers in John 17, in which we're invited into relational unity with God and each other. What a beautiful vision it is!

Some have promoted a very different view of God that compromises the historical and orthodox Christian understanding of the trinity. They say Jesus is "eternally subordinate" to God the Father. This position is then sometimes used to support the idea that women should live in permanent subordination to men. This claim is most unfortunate.

The "eternal subordination of the son" is a heresy that has been identified as such, beginning with the church father Athanasius in the fourth century. This heresy has often been called Arianism. The stakes are very high here as "the eternal subordination of the son" compromises a central tenant of the Christian faith regarding the very nature of God. For very good reasons, many Christian "complementarians" don't go this far. For further reading on this, I recommend Chapter 19 in the aforementioned book, *Discovering Biblical Equality: Complementary without Hierarchy.*

In Genesis 1-3, we see a beautiful vision for women and men who are equally and fully created in God's image to share life and mission together in unity. There is an absence of any God ordained vision for men to be in a position of power and authority over women. We also see a description of the tragic consequences of sin which includes the presence of a hierarchy of power that involves men having power over women. We also see a clue to the amazing relational nature of

God that we can emulate, as men and women, in our relationships with one another. All of this has crucial implications for men and women as they share life together in marriage, the church, and in society.

THE OLD TESTAMENT

Let's look at a few relevant passages from the Old Testament. As we look at the biblical message, it's important that we ask what did women in the Bible do? More specifically, what did these women do with the clear calling of God? What actions and deeds were clearly affirmed as valuable and led to blessings from God and the advancing of his kingdom?

We can find several examples of women in the Old Testament who were used by God in powerful ways, even as they served within a patriarchal context. Miriam was a prophet who spoke to the people with spiritual power (Exodus 15:20). She was a key leader who served with Moses and Aaron. People viewed her leadership with such high esteem that on one occasion they didn't want to move forward until she was ready to join them (Numbers 12:15). Her service and leadership are celebrated years later in the words of Scripture (Micah 6:4).

In II Kings 22:11-15, we find the people of Israel in crisis. King Josiah saw the need for a word from God. Many prominent male prophets were available and active at this time, but it was the female prophet Huldah who was sought out. After the king calls for her, she gives an authoritative word from God that led to powerful blessings.

When the king heard the words of the Book of the Law, he tore his robes. ¹² He gave these orders to Hilkiah the

priest, Ahikam son of Shaphan, Akbor son of Micaiah, Shaphan the secretary and Asaiah the king's attendant: ¹³ "Go and inquire of the LORD for me and for the people and for all Judah about what is written in this book that has been found. Great is the LORD's anger that burns against us because those who have gone before us have not obeyed the words of this book; they have not acted in accordance with all that is written there concerning us."

¹⁴ Hilkiah the priest, Ahikam, Akbor, Shaphan and Asaiah went to speak to the prophet Huldah, who was the wife of Shallum son of Tikvah, the son of Harhas, keeper of the wardrobe. She lived in Jerusalem, in the New Quarter.

¹⁵ She said to them, "This is what the LORD, the God of Israel, says:

For those who say God is opposed to women ever leading or teaching men, they must wrestle with this passage and the question: Why does God lead the king and priest to this woman to ask for and receive spiritual guidance and authoritative instruction?

In Judges 4-5, we read the amazing account of Deborah who was serving as the judge of Israel. From Judges 4:4:

Now Deborah, a prophet, the wife of Lappidoth, was leading Israel at that time.

Between the time of Joshua and the time Saul became king, Israel was led by judges. These judges served as the primary leaders for the nation of Israel as they gave judicial, political, administrative, and spiritual leadership. Deborah was the leader of Israel and served in this way. While leading the nation of Israel, one of Deborah's top military generals, Barak, said he would only go into battle if she would accompany him.

Barak said to her, "If you go with me, I will go; but if you won't go with me, I won't go. (Judges 4:8)

Deborah is chosen to lead the nation of Israel with no qualifying comment saying this was problematic or an undesirable exception. We see no comment saying this only happened because no man was willing or able to serve as the judge of Israel at this time. The Scriptures simply say she was the nation's leader, and as the story unfolds it is clear she led effectively and with God's blessing. Deborah's leadership in Judges 4-5 is a stunning description of a positive and effective female leader called and used by God in a powerful way.

The words of Deborah's song in Judges 5 are read and received as part of the authoritative Word of God we are called to hear and receive today. We might also consider the inspired words of Miriam, Hannah, and Mary in Scripture. If these words from women are part of God's very instruction in Scripture, why would we say women should not have an instructing voice in the church today? If these women's words are part of Scripture itself, how can we say we should limit the voice of women in the church today? It's confusing and problematic to say a woman's voice can be heard in Scripture as authoritative and valuable, but her voice should be restricted in the church today.

Other women also served God in word and deed in the Old Testament. Esther and Ruth certainly had an important part in God's mission. Deborah, Miriam, and the various female prophets stand out as examples of how women offered their leadership in service to God with his calling, gifting, and blessing.

JESUS AND THE GOSPELS

Jesus entered a world where women were marginalized and oppressed in multiple ways on a daily basis. Jesus models a vision for relational life between men and women that was confusing to many but was consistent with the vision we see in God's good creation. With the coming of Jesus Christ, the trajectory of God's revelation and work reaches a crucial point in a movement God had been guiding since creation and the fall. We see Jesus engaging with women in multiple ways and treating them with dignity and respect.

Consider how Jesus interacts with a woman in John 4. When the disciples left Jesus to go buy some food, Jesus met a Samaritan woman and engaged her in a lengthy conversation. It can be hard for us to understand, but at the time, it would have been virtually unthinkable that as a man and rabbi, Jesus would socially engage with a woman in this way. But we see in this simple act of entering this conversation, one of the most important implications of the gospel (the Good News). Jesus wanted to challenge the patriarchal values of the day and break down the barriers between men and women.

Jesus offers us a beautiful vision for human relationships. At the heart of this vision is this message: God created everyone in his image, everyone is loved by God, and everyone is offered forgiveness and the gift of salvation. Additionally, everyone is called to love everyone, always. Everyone is called and gifted to serve God in the mission of his church. The church will be a place where women and men, as well as people from various backgrounds, come together and experience unity in Christ as they love one another and serve God. Barriers and discrimination around race, class, gender, and nationality need to be removed in the power and vision of the gospel. We see Jesus breaking down these barriers throughout his ministry.

So, Jesus and his gospel extend a calling to all of us to get rid of our grudges, eradicate hatred from our heart, remove sexism, repent of our racism, let go of our petty political prejudices, stop marginalizing the poor, and refuse to let our nationalism outrank our citizenship in heaven. The way Jesus transforms our vision for people and relationships is good news indeed!

So, from now on we regard no one from a worldly point of view. Though we once regarded Christ in this way, we do so no longer. (II Corinthians 5:16)

The conversation Jesus had with this woman in John 4 was astounding. Women in his day typically had no or minimal educational opportunities and limited legal rights. As Jesus talked with this woman and his disciples processed their confusion, Jesus was modeling a beautiful vision for how to view women and share life with them.

Here are three phrases that were sometimes used by Jewish rabbis during the time Jesus lived, from William Barclay's *Commentary on John* (Chapter 4):

Let no one talk with a woman in the street, no, not with his own wife.

Better that the words of the law should be burned than delivered to a woman.

Each time a man prolongs a conversation with a woman he causes evil to himself.

In the world of Jesus, a common prayer Jewish boys were taught growing up and which men often continued to pray was this: "God, I thank you that you created me not as a gentile, a slave, or a woman." Jesus comes to a world where this demeaning perspective towards women was all too common. According to Barclay, in John 4, we see Jesus moving in a dramatically different direction:

By Rabbinic standards, Jesus could hardly have done a more shatteringly unconventional thing than to talk to this woman. Here is Jesus taking the barriers down.

When his disciples returned to Jesus, the Scriptures say they were **"surprised to find him talking with a woman"** (John 4:27). Jesus had indeed just concluded his longest one-on-one theological conversation we can find in the New Testament, and it was with a woman! Significantly, Jesus reveals to her that he is the Messiah. Following this conversation, she returns to her community and tells others about Jesus. John 4:38 says:

Many of the Samaritans from that town believed in him because of the woman's testimony.

Jesus is clearly fine with this woman being his emissary and instructing others about his identity in a way that led them into a new faith. Jesus didn't tell this woman not to speak or try to influence others because she was a woman. He didn't say this kind of instruction should only be given by men, nor did he tell her to limit her communication to women only. Her words were used by God to lead many people to faith.

Jesus not only talked with and listened to women, he allowed women in several settings to touch him with no rebuke or condemnation. In Luke 7, Jesus allows a woman to wash his feet with her hair. We read in Luke 7:44-48:

44 Then he turned toward the woman and said to Simon, "Do you see this woman? I came into your house. You did not give me any water for my feet, but she wet my feet with her tears and wiped them with her hair. 45 You did not give me a kiss, but this woman, from the time I entered, has not stopped kissing my feet. 46 You did not put oil on my head, but she has poured perfume on my feet. 47 Therefore, I tell you, her many sins have been forgiven—as her great love has shown. But whoever has been forgiven little loves little." 48 Then Jesus said to her, "Your sins are forgiven."

Jesus affirmed her faith, accepted her love, and set her free. This "sinful" woman was welcomed by Jesus while Simon was missing the point. In Luke 8:1-3 we read:

After this, Jesus traveled about from one town and village to another, proclaiming the good news of the kingdom of God. The Twelve were with him, and also some women who had been cured of evil spirits and diseases: Mary (called Magdalene) from whom seven

demons had come out; Joanna the wife of Chuza, the manager of Herod's household; Susanna; and many others. These women were helping to support them out of their own means.

We see here both men and women actively following their rabbi Jesus and traveling together. For Jesus to allow women to follow him in this way was unprecedented in the culture of his day. In Luke 10:38-42 we read:

38 As Jesus and his disciples were on their way, he came to a village where a woman named Martha opened her home to him. 39 She had a sister called Mary, who sat at the Lord's feet listening to what he said. 40 But Martha was distracted by all the preparations that had to be made. She came to him and asked, "Lord, don't you care that my sister has left me to do the work by myself? Tell her to help me!"

41 "Martha, Martha," the Lord answered, "you are worried and upset about many things, 42 but few things are needed—or indeed only one. Mary has chosen what is better, and it will not be taken away from her."

A specific observation of significance exists here with the reference to Mary as the one who "sat at the Lord's feet." This phrase was often used as a specific/technical reference to the way a student would learn from their rabbi. (Paul refers to this in Acts 22:3 when he talks about learning at the feet of Gamaliel.) To be described as "at the feet of a rabbi" was a way of identifying that person as a disciple of that rabbi. In Luke's description of Mary sitting at the feet of Jesus, we need to understand that for a woman to do this was unheard of in the Ancient Near East. We cannot find any historical record of a rabbi in Jesus's day having a female disciple.

Many read this passage and focus on the contrast in temperament displayed by Mary and Martha. We may find some value in this reflection, but that was not the cause of the tension in the room. In this first century context, it was stunning that Jesus welcomed a woman to sit at his feet with listening ears and an open heart. Mary was commended as one who was invited to learn from Jesus and be one of his disciples, even as he challenged the patriarchal values of the day. His actions were unprecedented, amazing, powerful, and beautiful!

One comment here on the twelve disciples: Some contend that because these twelve were men, this means the key leaders and pastors of any church need to be men. This misses the clear message throughout the Scriptures that affirms many women as key leaders in God's mission and movement in the world. If you follow this logic, we'd hear the case made that because the twelve disciples were Jewish, no Gentile should be in leadership.

Some have contended that Jesus chose twelve men because they represented the twelve tribes of Israel. Jesus was now reconstituting Israel under his leadership and these twelve represented the twelve sons of Jacob. Jesus was also living in such a patriarchal context that his selection of these twelve men likely made sense for a variety of reasons at that time. These factors shouldn't cause us to miss the many ways Jesus was moving people toward a new day when women would fully participate in his mission while serving in unity with their brothers.

When Jesus went to the cross, it was a group of women who were with him to the end. It was women who he first revealed himself to after his resurrection. One of the most important passages of Scripture on this whole subject can be found in Matthew 28 where we read:

So the women hurried away from the tomb, afraid yet filled with joy, and ran to tell his disciples. Suddenly Jesus met them. "Greetings," he said. They came to him, clasped his feet, and worshiped him. Then Jesus said to them, "Do not be afraid. Go and tell my brothers to go to Galilee; there they will see me." (Mathew 28:8-10)

At this time and place in history, women were often viewed as so unreliable and inferior to men that they were not even allowed to serve as witnesses in a court of law. Yet, these women were the first witnesses to the resurrection. The early church and the authors of the gospels stake the credibility of resurrection and the very integrity of their faith on the witness of these women. God chose to call and trust these women to be the first to declare the most important message the world would ever hear: "Jesus is alive!" If God trusted women to be the first to share the message of the resurrection, why would we restrict or limit their voice today? I appreciate this comment from Ron Sider in Chapter 18 of *How I Changed My Mind about Women in Leadership: Compelling Stories from Prominent Evangelicals*:

The conclusion seemed obvious to me: if the one I confessed as God Incarnate lived and taught the equality of women, I had better do the same.

I'm glad I follow a Savior who declared and modeled such a compelling vision. I'm grateful to follow a Lord who says to women: I want you to sit at my feet, hear my words, be my disciples, teach and lead others, worship me, and share my resurrection news with the world! I want you to be in the center of my church and in the middle of my mission.

THE EARLY NEW TESTAMENT CHURCH

As the New Testament church came to life, we find this description of followers of Jesus as they gathered together following the crucifixion, resurrection, and ascension of Jesus:

Then the apostles returned to Jerusalem from the hill called the Mount of Olives, a Sabbath day's walk from the city. When they arrived, they went upstairs to the room where they were staying. Those present were Peter, John, James, and Andrew; Philip and Thomas, Bartholomew and Matthew; James son of Alphaeus, and Simon the Zealot, and Judas son of James. They all joined together constantly in prayer, along with the women and Mary the mother of Jesus, and with his brothers. (Acts 1:12-14)

This occurs within a highly patriarchal culture where so often men and women were socially separated. Here we see women identified as a central and accepted part of the early church. This is consistent with how Jesus developed his community of followers. In Acts 2, we find a stunning account of how women were called to participate fully in God's mission.

Then Peter stood up with the Eleven, raised his voice, and addressed the crowd: "Fellow Jews and all of you who live in Jerusalem, let me explain this to you; listen carefully to what I say. [15] These people are not drunk, as you suppose. It's only nine in the morning! [16] No, this is what was spoken by the prophet Joel:

[17] "'In the last days, God says,

I will pour out my Spirit on all people.

Your sons and daughters will prophesy,

your young men will see visions,

your old men will dream dreams.

[18] Even on my servants, both men and women,

I will pour out my Spirit in those days,

and they will prophesy. (Acts 2:14-18)

At this historic moment when the Holy Spirt comes in a new and powerful way, what does God lead Peter to say? Of all the possible references to the Old Testament he could have mentioned, which one does he choose? Peter is inspired to proclaim the words of Joel that declare God's desire for women and men to proclaim his word together. As God empowers his church at Pentecost, the Spirit is given to both men and women who are called to declare God's word to the world.

It is clear something new, powerful, and exciting is happening here. God wants to use both women and men in prophetic ministry. To prophesy meant to speak an authoritative Word of God. To express a word of prophecy involved sharing words of inspiration and instruction. We cannot ignore or minimize the strategic importance of Pentecost and the way the Spirit was given to both men and women who were called to express prophetic messages in the very way the Old Testament prophet Joel predicted.

Women indeed prophesied in the early church. An example of this is found in Acts 21:8-9:

Leaving the next day, we reached Caesarea and stayed at the house of Philip the evangelist, one of the Seven. He had four unmarried daughters who prophesied.

Some will say the clear biblical message that God called and gifted women as prophets is not relevant when they restrict women from teaching or preaching. These individuals claim to serve as a prophet and give a prophetic word was a lesser function than teaching or preaching. This reflects a deeply problematic interpretation that misunderstands the power of the prophet and prophecy. The idea that prophecy did not involve authoritative words of inspiration and instruction misses the way prophecy was described in the New Testament itself. In II Corinthians 14:3-4 we read:

But the one who prophesies speaks to people for their strengthening, encouraging and comfort. Anyone who speaks in tongues edifies themselves, but the one who prophesies edifies the church.

I Corinthians 14:6 and 14:31 say:

Now, brothers and sisters, if I come to you and speak in tongues, what good will I be to you, unless I bring you

some revelation or knowledge or prophecy or word of instruction?

For you can all prophesy in turn so that everyone may be instructed and encouraged.

We see here that prophecy leads to learning. Both men and women have the ministry of instruction. The terms *prophet, teacher, instructor, preacher*, and so on each have a distinctive meaning. However, they also overlap in many ways. They are all part of the way God exhorts, encourages, instructs, inspires, and leads his people. In Acts 13:1, prophets and teachers seem to be viewed as one group. Observed by Klyne Snodgrass in his article, "A Case for the Unrestricted Ministry of Women":

I do not accept that the New Testament views prophecy and prophets as inferior to teaching and teachers.

God was calling women to be his voice to instruct and inspire people. People were being called to listen to women. At Pentecost, Peter was declaring with the support of the prophet Joel that a new day was coming alive in the church.

Another example of a woman, Priscilla, being used by God to instruct others and specifically instruct a man, Apollos, is found in Acts 18:24-26:

Meanwhile a Jew named Apollos, a native of Alexandria, came to Ephesus. He was a learned man, with a thorough knowledge of the Scriptures. He had been instructed in the way of the Lord, and he spoke with great fervor and taught about Jesus accurately, though he knew only the baptism of John. He began to speak

boldly in the synagogue. When Priscilla and Aquila heard him, they invited him to their home and explained to him the way of God more adequately.

One other quick observation and thought from the book of Acts.

But Saul began to destroy the church. Going from house to house, he dragged off both men and women and put them in prison. (Acts 8:3)

We don't have details on this of course, but as the early church gained momentum, it was clear the authorities were threatened. To try to crush the New Testament church, authorities typically imprisoned the leaders. It's significant that both men and women were put in jail for their faith. The fact that women were imprisoned by the opponents of Christianity speaks to their value in the church. If I'd had the opportunity to know these women, I'd have been eager to learn from them, serve with them, and followed those who were gifted leaders.

In Romans 16, we have a powerful description of people, both men and women, who the Apostle Paul served with and commends. I appreciate this statement from Pastor Gary Walter who served as president of the Evangelical Covenant Church:

As we read the entirety of Scripture, we are convinced the Bible normatively affirms women in leadership throughout both the Old and New Testaments. From Miriam and Deborah to Lydia and Priscilla – the stories of women in leadership are many. Of particular interest to me is Romans 16, where the Apostle Paul lists people of importance and influence, many of them women. There appears to be no distinction in leadership roles based on gender, notably listing Phoebe as a deacon and Junia as an apostle.

Romans 16:1 begins in this way:

I commend to you our sister Phoebe, a deacon of the church in Cenchreae. I ask you to receive her in the Lord in a way worthy of his people and to give her any help she may need from you, for she has been the benefactor of many people, including me.

The first phrase here is a greeting that was used to identify who brings the letter. Phoebe, a woman, is identified as the one Paul trusted to bring his letter to the church in Rome. In this role, she would be expected to represent the letter's sender and explain anything in the letter that needed clarification. This letter, like other New Testament letters, was most likely read to groups of people gathered together as a community. So, this woman would be the one who would be called on if any of the people in Rome wanted clarification regarding the letter's message. Paul is affirming Phoebe's role as a leader and as one who could instruct the church community.

Greet Andronicus and Junia, my fellow Jews who have been in prison with me. They are outstanding among the apostles, and they were in Christ before I was. (Romans 16:7)

Junia was a woman who is identified as an apostle. Some have tried to avoid the implications of this by saying it is unclear if Junia is actually a feminine name, but the vast majority of historical and biblical scholarship affirms Junia was a woman and that she was identified here as an apostle. Some have contended Junia was not really identified here as an apostle but was simply known by the apostles. This is a problematic interpretation that misses the clear message that Junia was an apostle and valued leader in the New Testament church.

Scot McKnight is an excellent New Testament scholar who has written an outstanding book, *Junia Is not Alone*, on this specific passage. If you're uncertain about how to understand this passage, I urge you to read this book. Romans 16 is a powerful passage showing us how the early church was living into God's vision for men and women serving their Lord together.

Again, what did women do in the Bible with the clear calling and blessing of God? Junia was a valued and dedicated leader in the church, a believer before Paul, imprisoned for her faith, and honored by Paul as an apostle. I'm confident both men and women who knew her were blessed by her service, faith, and leadership.

Women taught and led in the church because Jesus and his earliest followers clearly wanted this to be so. Unlike a world that viewed women as inferior and marginalized them in so many unfortunate ways, the church of Jesus Christ was striving to follow their master's example. The early church embraced a powerful vision that changed the way women were viewed and treated.

This surely was challenging, messy, and uncomfortable. The vision for men and women sharing life and ministry together as it was emerging in the New Testament church was a radical departure from society's norms. It must have been mind-bending for many of these early believers, who had grown up in such a patriarchal culture, to understand and embrace this vision. For men who grew up praying how grateful they were to not be "a women, slave, or gentile," this surely was a huge challenge.

But we see in this new community people beginning to share their Lord's values, follow his example, and live into the vision Peter declared at Pentecost. Gifted women began to serve as leaders in the church, and the mission moved forward in a stronger way through their dedicated service.

We hear this challenging and powerful declaration in Galatians 3:28:

There is neither Jew nor Gentile, neither slave nor free, nor is there male and female, for you are all one in Christ Jesus

This verse speaks to the comprehensive way the gospel of Jesus calls people into a new life and unique community. Barriers along the lines of ethnicity, class, and gender (which compromise the calling to justice, unity, and love) fade away in Christ. This verse is also understood as declaring the beauty of the new creation in Christ.

Some have contended that this verse speaks only to the opportunity for and experience of justification and salvation. They say Galatians 3:28 shouldn't be viewed as instructive on other issues such as our new life in Christ, relationships, or the mission of the church. I believe this perspective is flawed on many levels. Would people want to argue that this verse has nothing to say to us about race relations or how we view people who might be in a different economic class? Why do we try to minimize the power of what this is saying about the life men and women can experience together?

Paul was addressing false teaching among the Galatians and calling Jew and Gentile to live together in unity. We need to consider why Paul would add slave/free and male/female to his comments that were addressing the Jew/Gentile relationship. In Chapter 10 of *Discovering Biblical Equality: Complementarity without Hierarchy*, Gordon Fee summarizes this well by saying:

At issue, rather, for Paul is the passion of his life and calling: Jew and Gentile as one people of God in Christ. For him the crisis has to do with whether Gentiles get in on the promise to Abraham (Genesis 12:2-3; cf. Galatians 3:14) without also taking on Jewish identity, especially those marks of identity that specifically distinguished Jews from Gentiles in the Diaspora (circumcision, Sabbath and food laws). To put that in a more theological way, the driving issue in Galatians is not first of all soteriology but ecclesiology; who constitute the people of God in the new creation brought about by the "scandal of the cross" (Galatians 6:11-16)? ... What emerges in Paul's defense regarding the "truth of the gospel" (Galatians 2:5 & 14) are not terms like justification, faith, or works of the law. Rather, the overriding concern is for Gentile inclusion in the people of God.

We need to see how Galatians 3:28 is part of the biblical message of the new creation that is available in Christ (II Corinthians 5:11-21, Ephesians 2:14-16, Philippians 3:4-14). In the New Testament church, people where living into a new calling for relational life involving:

- The full inclusion of Gentiles in the church. (Acts 15)
- Slaves being viewed as fellow members of the Body of Christ. (Philemon)
- A citizenship in heaven that reshapes our understanding of our citizenship and role in any given nation. (Philippians 3:20)
- Men and women sharing life and ministry together in a new way. (Galatians 3:28, Romans 16, Acts 2:1-21)
- Authentic compassion for the poor, marginalized, and the hurting. (Matthew 25:31-46)
- The supremacy of love and grace following the model of our Lord. (Matthew 5:23-24, John 13:34-35, I Corinthians 13)

In Chapter 10 of *Discovering Biblical Equality: Complementarity without Hierarchy,* Fee summarizes this by saying:

It is this all-encompassing eschatological reality of "the new order," in which all these diverse expressions of being human are made one, that lies behind the remarkable addition of "slave nor free, ... male nor female" to "Jew nor Greek". ... Even though the categories themselves still function in the present, their significance in terms of old-age values has been abolished by Christ and the Spirit. ... And to give continuing significance to a male-authority viewpoint for men and women, whether at home or in the church, is to reject the new creation in favor of the norms of a fallen world.

. . .

A SUMMARY OF THE BIBLICAL MESSAGE ON WOMEN IN LEADERSHIP

God's good creation and intended best for humanity is reflected in Genesis 1-2. Men and women are equally and fully made in God's image and equally and fully called to rule over God's creation together. Men and women were created for community, living and serving in ways that reflect being made in the very image of God: Father, Son, and Holy Spirit. There is no hierarchy of male authority in God's good creation, and we should avoid imposing one in marriage, church, and society. The Bible describes a hierarchy of male authority and power over women in Genesis 3 and associates this directly with the tragedy of sin and human brokenness.

God clearly called, gifted, and used many women in the Old Testament as leaders who served God and his mission as they instructed, led, and blessed men and women in a variety of ways and settings.

Jesus demonstrates a beautiful way of viewing and treating women. He offers an inspiring vision when in a patriarchal cultural setting he honors and empowers women while welcoming them into his community. As a rabbi, Jesus invited women to be his disciples. Jesus ushers in a new movement where in relational life barriers of discrimination and exclusion based on race, class, nationality, and gender are challenged and broken down. This vision can guide us in our relationships in the church and beyond the church.

Women are the first ones entrusted with communicating the most important message the world would ever hear: Jesus has risen from the dead! (Matthew 28)

Women received the Holy Spirit with men at Pentecost. Peter proclaims this new movement of God was consistent with Old Testament prophecy and would involve women and men declaring God's message together in a powerful way. (Acts 2)

Many women were called and gifted by God in leading, teaching, and serving in the New Testament church. Phoebe is affirmed as a deacon and instructor in the church. Junia is identified and affirmed as an apostle. (Romans 16)

Paul referred to women as co-laborers and commends them for enduring imprisonment (Romans 16) while serving with them during his missionary journeys (Acts 18).

Many women were active as prophets in the New Testament church. (Acts 21:8-9)

Lydia appeared to be centrally involved in the beginning of the church in Philippi. (Acts 16)

Paul's bold declaration in Galatians 3:28 must be seen and received for what it is: a clear description of how, in Christ, we are part of a new community and new creation. There is no place for a hierarchy of power based on race, class, or gender in this new community. (Ephesians 2 and II Corinthians 5)

We see in Scripture a movement following "The Fall" in Genesis where God affirms and uses women in wonderful ways, even in settings that were steeped in patriarchal values. This trajectory of healing grace reaches a high point in the ministry of Jesus, Pentecost, and then in the many ways women served in all areas of life and leadership in the early New Testament church.

Following Jesus must involve embracing his vision for people and relational life. We also need to understand his calling to a different understanding and use of power. Jesus offers a challenging perspective that is saturated in his gospel with a calling to humility and service. In a world so often damaged by divisions and hierarchies that have led to discrimination and untold human suffering, Jesus proclaims a liberating way forward.

5

I TIMOTHY 2 AND I CORINTHIANS 11 & 14

Consider how we can best understand these two important passages of Scripture.

I TIMOTHY 2

People who believe women should be restricted from serving in leadership and support establishing a hierarchy of male authority in the church often point to I Timothy 2:8-15 to support their position. Let's take a look.

Therefore I want the men everywhere to pray, lifting up holy hands without anger or disputing. ⁹ I also want the women to dress modestly, with decency and propriety, adorning themselves, not with elaborate hairstyles or gold or pearls or expensive clothes, ¹⁰ but with good deeds, appropriate for women who profess to worship God.

¹¹ **A woman should learn in quietness and full submission. ¹² I do not permit a woman to teach or to assume authority over a man; she must be quiet. ¹³ For Adam was formed first, then Eve. ¹⁴ And Adam was not the one deceived; it was the woman who was deceived and became a sinner. ¹⁵ But women will be saved through childbearing—if they continue in faith, love and holiness with propriety.**

This is one of the more complex passages in the Bible. There is no shortage of biblical scholars who have offered various perspectives on its meaning. As I offer a few thoughts on this passage, I want us to keep this question in mind: Is this a temporary and local message best understood in the context of the moment and place it was written and received **OR** is this a universal and timeless command/prohibition for all places and all people?

Most people will quickly affirm that the directives given to women in 2:9 need to be understood as culturally conditioned with a limited literal application today. Does that same sensitivity apply to 2:12? I think it does. Also, saying this passage needs to be understood within its local context does not mean it has no value for us today. When we understand Scripture in light of its specific and original context, it helps us discover its meaning and identify appropriate applications for today.

Let's Remember:

This is a personal and pastoral letter. We need to recognize Paul's words here come in the form of a pastoral letter to a specific setting. Reading this letter is like listening to a phone conversation where you can only hear one person talking. There are limitations to the information we have, which should lead us to do our best to:

- Understand accurately what was happening in the context around the letter.
- Avoid reading something into the text that is simply not present.
- Look for the eternal truth and relevance of the passage without turning a word that might be addressing a specific local situation into a timeless command it was never intended to be.

Paul is addressing false teaching. Paul was writing primarily to urge Timothy to be alert to false teaching in the church. The call for prayer in 2:8 is likely connected to and informed by the call to prayer in 2:1. His concern was focused on women in the specific setting of Ephesus. It is likely some of these women were influenced by a female-led religious group in this city. Some may have been new believers who were influenced by this group and some form of false teaching that was associated with it (I Timothy 1:3 and 6:20-21). Since some may have contributed to the false teaching, it may have made sense for Timothy to urge them to let their faith develop before instructing others. It is reasonable to assume there were some specific things happening in Ephesus around false teaching that Paul's words were specifically addressing even if we don't have all the details.

The context in Ephesus was unique and surely shaped these specific instructions. Timothy was in Ephesus where the primary cultural and spiritual influence was centered on the temple of Diana, which was led by female priests. In this setting, people were called to worship a female goddess who was believed to be the goddess of childbirth. The temple of Diana was considered one of the seven wonders of the ancient world. The influence of this temple and religious group was strong.

It is likely Paul was troubled by the practices and teachings of this temple. His word to Timothy may have been addressing specific issues associated with the temple in ways we cannot be certain of, but which were very specific to Timothy's setting. Perhaps women were being converted and were trying to sort out their new faith in Christ in the context of previously held beliefs. If some of these new believers had been leaders and teachers in the temple of Diana, it is possible Paul wanted them to slow down and learn more before they began to teach others in the church. He also may have wanted to help these women avoid any appearances that might cause people to identify them as followers of this local temple group.

The unique context around the female-led temple of Diana certainly could be part of what Paul is addressing here, especially given his clear concern for false teaching. Given this, it isn't wise to take these words to be a universal rule about all women being prohibited from ever being in a position of church leadership in any time, way, or setting.

These instructions were likely given to help women avoid being associated with the followers of the temple of Diana or being viewed as prostitutes. It is also possible that, in some way, these words were given to help women who were coming out of the unique Ephesus temple community to disassociate themselves from their previous temple allegiance and practices.

It is significant that Paul is urging (even commanding, as this verb is in the imperative form) women to learn in a society in which women typically had no educational opportunities. This calling for women to learn is a strong word of affirmation regarding their value and dignity. The submission mentioned here should not be assumed to mean submission to male authority. The call to submission is most likely to the process of learning, to the Lord, and/or to the truth of the gospel. This calling to learn in submission could certainly apply to men as well when understood as a call to learn with humility and a teachable spirit.

The language was specific and significant. In 2:12, the Greek word used for authority is unique – *authentein* – and is not used in any other place in the New Testament. Paul's unusual use of this word would suggest he had a specific purpose in mind to address a specific situation. *Authentein* often meant to dominate another, even in a violent way. In 2:12, Paul was not talking about how to lead with healthy authority. He was addressing and condemning an unhealthy "dominating" use of force that was apparently present in Ephesus.

It is most likely Paul knew of a specific challenge Timothy was dealing with among the women in Ephesus and so he addresses the *authentein* in a unique and strong way. Some women, who may have been influenced by the temple practices in Ephesus, may have been domineering in their teaching and relationships. Given the specific meaning of this word and its unique use in this context, it is inappropriate to apply this verse as a rationale for restricting women from ever offering healthy teaching or leadership. Healthy and normal teaching and leadership in the church are not what is being addressed here. The language makes it clear Paul was prohibiting a domineering spirit and harsh method of instruction.

I contend this instruction could be given to men as well when properly understood as a call to avoid the misuse of power. Many biblical scholars have struggled with how to translate this passage. As we understand the word *authentein,* it is quite reasonable to conclude Paul may have been saying: "I do not permit a woman to teach with a vision to dominate a man," or "I do not permit a woman to dominate a man," or "I do not permit a woman to teach a man in a domineering way."

Another variable in translation is around the tense of the word "permit." When Paul says, "I do not permit," some believe a more accurate translation would be, "I do not now permit." It points to this being best understood as a specific word with a local application rather than a timeless universal command.

Some thoughts on the words regarding Genesis. The words looking back to Genesis are complex. Because Paul refers to creation at this point, some contend the text becomes a universal instruction. We need to remember Paul occasionally refers to creation and he does this in a variety of ways (Romans 5:12-21, II Corinthians 11:3, I Timothy 4:1-5).

The meaning of the order of creation is a question that needs to be understood within a larger study of the whole of Scripture. Nowhere in Scripture is there an explicit teaching that establishes patriarchy as a divine order that reflects God's will for his creation. We certainly cannot find any teaching regarding the creation order as giving support to this. So, to use this one verse to create a universal command is a problematic and weak foundation for such a theological construct.

When interpreting Scripture, it's wise to let the "big" help us understand the "small" and not build a large position on a small biblical foundation. It is also unreasonable to conclude either Eve or Adam is more responsible for the original fall in Genesis. The overall message of Scripture is men and women are both complicit in "The Fall" and both can be fully saved by grace.

If we try and interpret these verses in a purely literal way independent of context sensitivities, we could argue this passage (2:15) is saying because women are saved through childbirth, women who cannot become pregnant are not eligible for salvation. I'm not saying that! Rather, I'm illustrating the problems with isolating and interpreting a specific sentence in a literal way independent of the context. It is very possible this childbirth reference was intended to be understood in connection with a common belief in Ephesus that the temple goddess would assist women in childbirth. Paul may have been encouraging women to know they don't need the goddess from the temple in Ephesus to get them through childbirth.

We need to understand I Timothy 2 in light of the preponderance of biblical evidence. We have only a partial understanding of what Paul and Timothy were addressing in their own situation. While we strive to accurately understand the context, we also remember that when people exchange letters there is a measure of shared background and information that informs the meanings of the letter, which an independent reader simply has no access to. All this leads me to avoid interpreting and applying this word in a literal way to every person or setting throughout history, just as most people avoid doing this with I Timothy 2:9.

I have talked with people who quote I Timothy 2:12 and say: "This is so obvious and clear, women shouldn't be allowed to teach or to lead men." What they often don't realize is they (wisely) don't interpret other portions of Scripture in this way.

From previous examples, most people understand it is simplistic and problematic to isolate specific quotes and their literal interpretation. For example, it is problematic to isolate:

- I Corinthians 16:20 ... and demand that we always greet people today with a holy kiss.
- Mark 10:21 ... and say every Christian should sell everything they have and then give all their money to the poor.
- Matthew 5:27-29 ... and cut your eyes out if you have a moment of sexual lust.
- I Timothy 5:23 ... and tell everyone to drink wine for your health.

- Matthew 6:6 ... and never pray with other people and only pray in private.
- Luke 14:26 ... and say to be a follower of Jesus you must hate your parents.

In the same way, it is simplistic and problematic to isolate I Timothy 2:12 apart from the whole of Scripture and try to understand it using a literal method of interpretation we would never use with the verses above.

We also must read I Timothy 2 alongside the many passages in the Bible where we see God call and gift women to lead and teach. Let's remember:

- Paul often describes women as co-laborers without any reference to a subordinate position due to their gender.
- Paul calls people in Philippians 2 to submit to one another without any qualification about women submitting to men. This indeed is best understood as a call to a spirit and practice of submission in all our relationships.
- If the comments Paul makes about women's behavior in verses 9-10 are culturally conditioned, we should be open to this same dynamic being present in some way in verse 12.
- Romans 16 gives us powerful evidence for the way God called and used women in leadership in the church.
- Pentecost and Peter clearly declare God's vision for women and men to both declare God's word.

I Timothy 2 is a complex passage that is best understood as we consider the specific situation Paul was addressing. It should not be used as a timeless and universal command that prohibits any woman from ever offering teaching and leadership in the church. This does not mean this passage has no value for us today. We see in this text wise words that can be helpful in so many situations today as we think about the calling to:

- Avoid teaching anyone in a domineering way (*authentein*).
- Pay attention to how your conduct could represent the gospel and the church.
- Be sure you have reached an appropriate level of learning and maturity before teaching others.
- Learn with a humble and teachable spirit.
- Encourage women to learn.
- Avoid worshiping false gods who won't help you with childbirth or anything else.

I appreciate these words.

The prohibition in I Timothy 2 was required by conditions in that time and place. ... These words should not be used as a universal prohibition of teaching by women. (Klyne Snodgrass in "The Biblical & Theological Basis for Women in Ministry")

I Timothy 2:11-12 is not a timeless, transcultural absolute for the place of women in the church, but rather a specific qualified response to a particular historical situation. (David Scholer, *Covenant Companion Magazine*, 1984)

Galatians 3:28 makes it clear that all believers are on the same level in the church, and there is no hierarchy that places all women below all men ... The teaching of I Timothy 2 must have been for a special situation where teaching and leadership by women were causing temporary, local problems. (Howard Marshall in Chapter 11 of *How I Changed My Mind about Women in Leadership: Compelling Stories from Prominent Evangelicals)*

I CORINTHIANS 11 & 14

[2] **I praise you for remembering me in everything and for holding to the traditions just as I passed them on to you. [3] But I want you to realize that the head of every man is Christ, and the head of the woman is man, and the head of Christ is God. [4] Every man who prays or prophesies with his head covered dishonors his head. [5] But every woman who prays or prophesies with her head uncovered dishonors her head—it is the same as having her head shaved. [6] For if a woman does not cover her head, she might as well have her hair cut off; but if it is a disgrace for a woman to have her hair cut off or her head shaved, then she should cover her head.**

[7] **A man ought not to cover his head, since he is the image and glory of God; but woman is the glory of man. [8] For man did not come from woman, but woman from man; [9] neither was man created for woman, but woman for man. [10] It is for this reason that a woman ought to have authority over her own head, because of the angels. [11] Nevertheless, in the Lord woman is not independent of man, nor is man independent of woman. [12] For as woman came from man, so also man is**

born of woman. But everything comes from God. (I Corinthians 11:2-12)

Women should remain silent in the churches. They are not allowed to speak, but must be in submission, as the law says. If they want to inquire about something, they should ask their own husbands at home; for it is disgraceful for a woman to speak in the church. (I Corinthians 14:34-35)

Portions of I Corinthians 11 and 14 are sometimes used to support the position that women should be restricted in their service and leadership in the church. Here are a few thoughts about this.

In I Corinthians, we see a reference to a man being the "head" of a woman. This word has been interpreted in many ways and much debated. Many conclude the Greek word for head here – *kephale* – has the meaning of "source." This presents a different meaning from the way this word is some-times used in English to mean "authority over." Again, this has been much debated and it is difficult to be 100 percent certain how this word was understood in this passage by Paul and the first readers in Corinth.

The biblical teaching on "headship" is small and very limited. While we shouldn't ignore it, we should recognize its complexity. Regardless of how one interprets the meaning of "head" in the New Testament, I believe it is very possible Paul is making a reference to how things generally were in that day. He was acknowledging a cultural reality. Doing this is not the same as declaring this is God's best intention for humanity. This is similar to the way people have wrestled with the biblical teachings on slavery. We understand that Paul can give instructions that relate to a cultural reality to help people live within that reality without assuming he is thus endorsing that cultural structure or condition as God's will for people.

It is entirely possible that Paul is acknowledging the Corinthians were living in a society where the husband most often did rule over his wife – just as masters ruled over slaves – without saying or teaching that this social system is the best expression of God's will. (John Ortberg, Willow Creek Church Leadership Seminar)

In Chapter 21 of *Discovering Biblical Equality: Complementarity without Hierarchy*, Gordon Fee expresses this perspective as well:

Paul thus assumes a Greco-Roman patriarchal culture when he instructs Christians how to live within it ... but he does not thereby bless the culture itself ... There is no question that these texts reflect the patriarchal worldview of the Greco-Roman world, but they do not bless that worldview theologically. Rather, Paul's instructions (like Peter's in I Peter 2:18-3:7) have to do with how to live out the life of Christ in such a cultural setting.

In Ephesians 5, Paul uses the word "head" as he calls husbands to embrace their responsibilities well in a patriarchal world, but this does not mean patriarchy is specifically endorsed. For a helpful discussion of this topic and the biblical understanding of "head," I would recommend *Ephesians (The NIV Application Commentary Book 10)* by Klyne Snodgrass. In his discussion of Ephesians 5 and headship in marriage Klyne Snodgrass offers this helpful perspective:

Does this text have relevance for decisions about the role of women and ministry? The answer is "no," except for the fact that mutual submission gives all persons equal value. The passage is about mutual submission and family relationships, not about church leadership and what women may or may not do."

We would do well to remember the words in I Corinthians 11:11-12. This is a beautiful expression of how the shared equality and interdependence of people as male and female can be understood.

Nevertheless, in the Lord woman is not independent of man, nor is man independent of woman. For as woman came from man, so also man is born of woman. But everything comes from God.

In I Corinthians 14, there is a focus on the church's apparently chaotic worship services. From 14:26, we can see that disruptions in the Corinthian church worship services were clearly being addressed. The statement about women being silent most likely flowed from Paul's understanding of a specific situation in the Corinthians public worship gatherings. Women may have been disruptive in some way and that's what he's addressing here, but we don't have the details.

We also need to remember the clear statement in I Corinthians 11 that women were present and active in sharing public prayers and prophecies. There are challenges to understanding how the instructions in Chapters 11 and

14 fit together. One would have to say Paul is contradicting himself if I Corinthians 14 is used to promote the idea women cannot speak in the church, while also talking about women who pray and prophesy in worship in Chapter 11. Paul clearly seems to be addressing a specific situation in the worship services of the Corinth church. It is unreasonable to understand this passage as a timeless and universal statement that women cannot speak, teach, preach, or prophesy in any church, in any location, and at any time.

As we sometimes struggle with understanding some of Paul's words, we might find some encouragement from Peter, who seemed to struggle with this as well. Peter writes in II Peter 3:15-16:

Just as our dear brother Paul also wrote you with the wisdom God gave him. He writes the same way in all his letters, speaking in them of these matters. His letters contain some things that are hard to understand...

This does not mean we can't understand anything, live with gracious conviction, or that we give up on the vital work of exploring the Scriptures. For myself, these words encourage me to be humble and accept the reality that some things in Scripture are indeed difficult to understand. When I wrestle with portions of Scripture that are more complex and difficult to understand, Peter's words also move me to keep the larger themes of the gospel and Scripture in focus.

I appreciate these reflections on I Corinthians 14:34-35 and I Timothy 2:11-12 from Ron Sider in Chapter 18 of *How I Changed My Mind about Women in Leadership: Compelling Stories from Prominent Evangelicals*:

To this day, I do not feel certain that I fully understand them. But since the broad sweep of revelation history moves from equality at creation through terrible brokenness in male-female relationships because of the fall to a radical departure in Jesus and the early church from typical first-century male prejudice against women, I conclude that these two texts probably refer to some local situation rather than a universal norm.

6

SLAVERY: A RELEVANT PARALLEL

We hold that the issue of gender inclusiveness for the present generation of evangelical Christians is a near-identical parallel to that of slavery for the 19th century.

—Alan Johnson, *How I Changed My Mind about Women in Leadership: Compelling Stories from Prominent Evangelicals (Introduction)*

We can see how the story of slavery in America offers a relevant parallel to the issue of women in leadership in the church today as we ask these questions: Can the church be wrong? Can we have a blind spot? How do we use Scripture? Is there a power parallel? Can we change?

Slavery is a classic and tragic example of how some people approached the Scriptures and failed to remember the big picture. Too often, they isolated a few verses of Scripture and interpreted them in a literal and ultimately simplistic, superficial, and problematic way. Unfortunately, in many places for many years, Christian leaders justified slavery as an institution, claiming slavery was supported by the Bible. They said slavery was endorsed by the clear teaching of Scripture. This reflects a heartbreaking misunderstanding of biblical teaching. Fortunately, over time, this perspective changed, and Christians often led the abolitionist movement to end slavery.

How did the church change from using the Bible to support slavery to appealing to Scripture as a basis to abolish it?

This change occurred over time as people took a fresh look at Scripture and came to a new understanding. To justify slavery in the name of biblical truth was tragic and driven by selfishness and sin. It was also the result of sloppy practices of biblical interpretation. This resulted in a Christian consensus in some areas (especially in Southern states) that claimed the Bible supported slavery. This occurred as people focused on a few isolated verses, misunderstood them in their specific context, and ignored the larger biblical themes of the gospel itself and God's redemptive mission.

Fortunately, today there is an overwhelming consensus in the Christian Church that slavery is evil. In response to the Spirit's leading and the biblical message, many Christian people, and the church, are on the front lines of fighting modern day slavery/human trafficking.

Consider these verses from the Bible.

Slaves, in reverent fear of God submit yourselves to your masters, not only to those who are good and

considerate, but also to those who are harsh. (I Peter 2:18)

Slaves, obey your earthly masters in everything; and do it, not only when their eye is one you and to curry their favor, but with sincerity of heart and reverence for the Lord. (Colossians 3:22)

Slaves, obey your masters with respect and fear, and with sincerity of heart, just as you would obey Christ. (Ephesians 6:5)

For many years and in many places, especially in the 1700s and 1800s in the United States, some looked at these verses and concluded: It's simple! It is crystal clear. Just look at the clear teaching of Scripture. Slavery is never specifically condemned, and slaves are urged to be obedient to their masters. It is clear the Bible supports slavery.

The people who supported slavery in the name of biblical Christianity isolated a few verses like these and built a whole case for something that was inconsistent with the larger redemptive message of the gospel. They also read the Scriptures *through* their tradition rather than *with* their tradition. Frankly, they were also blinded by their own sin, thirst for power, racism, greed, and self-interest.

The supporters of slavery were vulnerable to believing the Bible was saying what they wanted it to say in order for them to maintain a position of power and economic advantage over others. This historical example is both sobering and tragic. It should challenge us to be very careful if we use the Bible to justify creating a hierarchy that allows us to hold a position of power over others.

But history also shows that Christian people and church leaders, such as William Wilberforce, Charles Finney, and Charles Wesley, led the fight for abolition in response to the gospel and biblical teaching. A different voice began to gain momentum as many people looked at the Scriptures and began to see:

- The Bible clearly says everyone is created in God's image and loved by God.
- Does not the supreme call to love challenge the whole concept of slavery?
- Slaves in the New Testament were part of the church. They were identified as fellow believers with an equal standing before God and others.
- Many of the Old Testament prophets and Jesus himself were clear in their concern for the marginalized and the oppressed.
- In the book of Acts, we see a new community emerging with many barriers among different groups coming down.
- The brief book of Philemon shares a big message about how a slave needs to be viewed as a fellow believer.
- The movement of the church in the book of Acts, the letter of Philemon, and Galatians 3:28 needed be heard along with the verses that seemed to support slavery.
- Perhaps we need to rethink how we understand biblical references to an institution like slavery and not assume these references are an endorsement of slavery. These verses should be understood as

helping people to live within the reality of slavery
but not as words of support for slavery itself.

As people prayed and studied the Scriptures with an open heart, the Spirit began to move. People's blind spot of supporting slavery in the name of biblical Christianity began to be reevaluated. Studying Scripture in its context was valued. Isolating a small portion of Scripture to justify a position, while ignoring the heart of the Biblical message, was identified as problematic.

The example of slavery is both disturbing and hopeful. It can show us how easy it can be to develop a blind spot and make the Bible say what we want it to say. However, it is hopeful as we see how people changed their mind as they continued to come back to the Biblical message.

In drawing this parallel between slavery and the question of women in leadership in the church, I am certainly not saying people who want to restrict women are also supporters of slavery. I am saying that how the church wrestled with the issue of slavery offers us a relevant and revealing parallel as we think about understanding the biblical message regarding women in leadership in the church.

Slavery can be a relevant parallel as we see how:

The church can be wrong. There have been times when the church has believed something for a long time and been mistaken. We must recognize we might be wrong, even if our beliefs are affirmed by many people in our church or social context. Let's consider this when those who support restricting women from leadership in the church tell us we should hold that position because it's been widely held for many years among many people.

We can have a "blind" spot. We're all capable of missing things. It's hard to be objective. We can be certain of something, but simply be mistaken. I respectfully contend that those who advocate for the restrictive position regarding women in leadership have a blind spot that needs to be reevaluated.

The methods of biblical interpretation are similar. The way pro-slavery Christians approached the process of biblical interpretation was virtually identical to the way many today use the Scriptures to justify restricting women from leadership in the church.

This was and is a power issue. As the saying goes, power can corrupt; absolute power often corrupts absolutely. There is no doubt many who defended slavery were trying to justify their positions of power. The issue of restricting or not restricting women from leadership is also a power issue. Jesus cautions us regarding the deceptive allure of power. He encourages people to serve one another and follow his example of service (Mark 10:45 and Matthew 21:26-28). We should be careful if we find ourselves using the Bible to establish power over others.

Change can happen. It can be hard to change our mind and position, and it often involves needed humility and even repentance. But change can happen and is often valuable and good.

When we consider the similar methods of biblical interpretation among those who used the Bible to justify slavery and those doing the same to justify restricting women, I appreciate Beth Allison Barr's perspective in Chapter 1 of *The Making of Biblical Womanhood: How the Subjugation of Women Became Gospel Truth*:

When we rightly understand that the biblical passages discussing slavery must be framed within their historical context and that, through the lens of historical context, we can better see slavery as an ungodly system that stands contrary to the gospel of Christ, how can we not then apply the same standards to the biblical texts about women?

In the book *How I Changed My Mind about Women in Leadership: Compelling Stories from Prominent Evangelicals*, approximately twenty Christian leaders share their stories of personal transformation. They describe how God moved them from holding the **restrictive/complementarian** position to changing their minds and becoming advocates of biblical equality while holding the **non-restrictive/egalitarian** position. Among these contributors are two who offer these powerful reflections on how slavery is a relevant parallel when thinking about women in leadership (Chapters 7 and 15).

From Stan Gundry, pastor, seminary professor, and leader with the Zondervan Corporation:

In early 1974 I was preparing for a doctoral field exam in American church history by reading selections from some of the more important primary source documents representative of that history. When I came to the early and mid-nineteenth century, I was immersed in the literature surrounding the questions of slavery and abolition. The defenses of slavery by leading theologians and churchmen from the southern states were especially fascinating. Whether the men were from the Baptist, Presbyterian, Episcopal, Congregational, or Roman Catholic traditions, the biblical and theological arguments in defense of slavery were essentially the same.

Abolitionism was said to be anti-Christian. Defenders of slavery claimed that abolitionists got their ideas from other sources and then went to the "Bible to confirm the crotchets of their vain philosophy." Scripture, it was repeatedly argued, does not condemn slavery. In fact, Scripture sanctions slavery. In his parables, Jesus refers to masters and slaves without condemning slavery as such. In the New Testament, pious and good men had slaves, and they were not told to release them. The church was first organized in the home of a slaveholder. That slavery was divinely regulated throughout biblical history was evidence that the institution was divinely approved. When Scripture, as in Galatians 4, uses illustrations from slavery to teach great truths without censuring slavery, it was considered more evidence that the institution had divine approval. The Baptist Declaration of 1822 did accept that slaves had purely spiritual privileges (as Christians), but they remained slaves.

The defenders of slavery within the churches all claimed the Bible as their starting point, and all developed their defense by appealing to Scripture in much the fashion I have summarized above. With one voice Southern churchmen defending slavery charged that to reject slavery as sinful was to reject the Word of God.

I had heard about this line of reasoning before, but to actually read it for myself was an eye-opening experience. I was appalled and embarrassed that such an evil practice had been defended in the name of God and under the guise of biblical authority. How could churchmen and leading theologians have been so foolish and blind? I had been reflecting on these readings several days; then on one, cold, Chicago-gray wintry day as I crept home on that parking lot known as the Eisenhower Expressway, it slowly began to dawn on me that I had heard every one of those arguments before. In fact, at one time I had used them—to defend hierarchicalism and argue against egalitarianism. By this time I was close to home and I still remember the exact spot on Manchester Road just west of downtown Wheaton, Illinois, where it hit me like a flash. Someday Christians will be as embarrassed by the church's biblical defense of patriarchal hierarchicalism as it is now of the nineteenth century biblical defense of slavery.

From Cornelius Plantinga, pastor and professor at Calvin Theological Seminary:

What could be clearer, the southerners asked? You northerners might think that God is against slavery, but God's Word says otherwise. God's Word treats the duties of slaves as naturally as it treats the duties of children and wives. They are to submit. How could God's Word enjoin slave submission if it were immoral? How could slavery violate the Golden Rule or the commandment to love neighbors if the same Bible tells Israel to buy slaves, treats slavery as a normal part of life, and tells slaves to obey their masters as the Lord?

I found myself at a crossroad. All along, I had wanted both gender egalitarianism and also faithfulness to the plain teaching of the female subordination texts in especially 1 Corinthians 11 and 14 and 1 Timothy 2. I had seen no way to get these things together. I had to go with Scripture.

But then, that snowy afternoon in 1970 it hit me with the force of a revelation that the female subordination texts and the slave subordination texts were in the same hermeneutical boat. The texts were sometimes in the same book of the Bible or even in the same chapter. In both cases you could maintain an egalitarian position only by going to the spirit of the Bible, the general direction of the Bible, the doctrine of the image of God in the Bible, the majestic assertion of the Bible that in Christ "there is neither Jew nor Greek, slave nor free, male nor female, for you are all one in Christ Jesus" (Galatians 3:28).

With respect to the slave subordination texts, everybody I knew did this without distress. I couldn't think of even one conservative Christian who thought the slave subordination texts still applied to Christian slaves today (of which there are all too many). I wondered by what hermeneutic such Christians were able to finesse or relativize the slave subordination texts while insisting on the enduring application of the female subordination texts that came from the same neighborhood in the Bible?

Still today, gender subordinationists say they are only bowing to the authority of Scripture, which requires (asymmetric) female subordination in at least 1 Corinthians 11 and 14 and 1 Timothy 2. But, of course, the same Bible also requires the subordination of slaves. We do not. We heartily approve slave rescue, slave escape, and other slave insubordinations. Gender subordinationists typically reply that this is an unfair comparison; after all, they say, slavery is a product of our fallenness whereas the subordination of women is part of creation. Thinking about this over the years, I have not been able to believe that this last statement about created female subordina-

tion is true, and I do not believe that it is based on a discerning reading of Scripture.

Nonetheless, however firm the biblical ties that bind slaves to their masters, virtually every modern Christian relativizes them. They do not apply to us any longer. What is crucial to see is that the hermeneutical justification for such a move will be impressively similar to the justification for relativizing the gender subordination commands. Namely, in both cases we would look for justification to the bigger patterns of the events of Christ and the Spirit and the constitutive and summary statements of the significance of these events—both of which give us purchase on the direction of God's redemptive program.

Jesus was sent "to proclaim freedom for the prisoners and ... to release the oppressed" (Luke 4:18). At Pentecost sons and daughters, male and female slaves—all are inspired to proclaim God's Word. Worldly people may suppress women, yet "in the Lord ... woman is not independent of man, nor is man independent of woman" (1 Corinthians 11:11). Devout Jewish men may have thanked God every morning that they were not a Gentile, nor a slave, nor a woman, but in Christ the subordination ironed into these distinctions has been rendered antique.

The upshot is that it is remarkably hard to dismiss what Paul says to slaves. You need a big, subtle hermeneutic to do it. You need one just like that used by gender egalitarians. You need to be able to tell time, theologically. You need to see the big movement of the history of redemption that rises above the small print for local times and places.

F. F. Bruce, a world-class Paulinist of impeccable evangelical credentials, once made a telling remark in this connection. After stressing that Galatians 3:28 and kindred passages are the "foundation principles" of Paul's teaching in the light of which problem passages on female subordination must be understood, Bruce added this: "In general, where there are divided opinions about the interpretation of a Pauline passage, that interpretation which runs along the line of liberty is much more likely to be true to Paul's intention than one which smacks of bondage or legalism.

Given the almost universal sexism of first-century settings, the preaching and ruling of women might then have been scandalous and detrimental to the preaching of the gospel. Today the situation is precisely reversed. It is the exclusion of women—often done with lofty and humorless reassurances that they are equal even if subordinate—that is scandalous and enervating ... the policy of excluding women has become deeply embarrassing. Males discuss somberly whether we ought to "allow" women into church offices. The discussion sounds so much like that of parents trying to decide whether their adolescents are ready to assume adult responsibilities. It sounds so much like majorities dithering over whether they ought to invite minorities into their club. It sounds as if the church belongs to males.

I know, of course, that decisions based on the spirit of Scripture, the sweep of Scripture, the direction of Scripture rather than on the "plain" teachings of individual texts make a lot of us evangelicals antsy. They make me antsy. Isn't that how you get theological and moral liberalism out of the Bible? Just generalize up a few levels till you get to your comfort zone and call it biblical.

But any of us who relativizes the slave subordination commands in the New Testament has already been walking that path. We are embarked. We reject slavery not because individual texts condemn it, but because the sweep of Scripture does. Most of us evangelicals are so convinced that slavery is wicked that Ephesians 6:5 & co. will not move us. The text must have had local and temporary application. We think that if in Sudan today a Christian were kidnapped, sold into slavery, and forbidden to escape by his master, his Christian duty should not be determined simply by reading Ephesians 6:5.

Seeing this one snowy day in 1970 permanently changed my mind about women in church leadership. And I'm glad it did. To me, the advent of women in church leadership has been one of the most precious gifts of God in my lifetime.

7

CHURCH OFFICES AND CHURCH HISTORY

Consider the following reflections on Church offices and history and how they influence our understanding of men and women's service in the church.

CHURCH STRUCTURE AND MINISTRY OFFICES

How we understand the New Testament church organizational structure and use of authority can influence how we understand what the Bible teaches about women in leadership in the church. Some say only men served in the "office" of pastor in the early church and so we should follow this pattern.

Here are my thoughts.

- We can find no clear teaching in the Bible about church government and structure, nor any evidence of a common or clear model of church organization or ministry offices. The church was an emerging reality when the New Testament was written. Many of these churches were small groups meeting in homes just trying to figure out how to live out their new life and mission in Christ. There were no buildings, budgets, church constitutions, pulpits, seminaries, denominations, policies, or organizational structures. With no clear instruction on this subject, we should not impose any structure of church offices or form of church governance as clearly biblical. With no clear biblical evidence, we should avoid turning a spiritual gift (e.g., pastor, teacher, leader) into some type of "office" only men can hold when there is no clear biblical evidence for this.

- We see no clear indication that the earliest church communities were led by individual pastors. Paul's letters to specific church communities were most often addressed to a group. There often seemed to be a plurality of leadership. While Paul and others moved around to various churches to offer encouragement, the idea of the individual pastor had not clearly taken shape. No evidence exists addressing a specific role of "Senior Pastor." (Interestingly, II John is one letter that many believe was addressed to a specific individual who was the leader of a church, to an elder who was female.)

- There was no common language or understanding for church "offices" in the New Testament church. Numerous words were used describing spiritual gifts and people who served in certain ways such as shepherd, pastor, evangelist, elder, overseer, apostle, deacon, teacher, leader, etc. These terms often overlapped and do not describe an "office."

- The Old Testament priesthood is not the model for Christian ministry today. Any reference to this as a justification for restricting women reflects a misunderstanding of or lack of belief in what many Christians call "The Priesthood of all Believers". This concept began to gain support in Europe during the reformation in the 1500s and declares all believers are called and gifted to know and serve God. (See I Peter 2:9)

- Pentecost changes everything. The Spirit gifts people as the Spirit desires. Men and women are both clearly gifted for ministry. None of the key New Testament passages that describe spiritual gifts indicate that any of these gifts are given only to men or to be used exclusively by men (Romans 12, Ephesians 4, I Corinthians 12). As we saw earlier, at Pentecost in Acts 2, Peter declares that men and women are called to carry the mission of the church forward together as they are empowered by the Holy Spirit.

- We also need to pay attention to the strong teachings of Jesus regarding power and service. When the disciples argued about who would be the greatest within their group, Jesus taught them to be servants with a humble spirit (Mark 9:33-35 and Luke 22:24-27). We need to ask how much of the resistance to sharing church leadership with women reflects a struggle with control and giving up power?

- The book *Discovering Biblical Equality: Complementarity without Hierarchy* contains excellent chapters (14, 15, 16) on this subject and the nature of authority in the early church. This resource is helpful in exploring a biblical vision for authority that doesn't place power exclusively with men. Authority is in the gospel and in Jesus himself, not in any specific office or individual person.
- From the Covenant Church Theological Symposium (2018), Klyne Snodgrass offers this thought: *The real problems are not I Corinthians 14 and I Timothy 2, but an illegitimate understanding of authority and wrong assumptions about church office. The NT does not connect authority with church teaching. The only time authority (exousia) is used in connection with teaching is with the teaching of Jesus.... The NT understanding of authority is crucial. It is the authority of the gospel, not the authority of an office or person. ... The gospel requires a new understanding and implementation of power. The real issue is power.*

I reject the idea that the New Testament teaches there are ministry positions or offices that can only be held by men. There is no specific form of church government that is clearly identified or even described as the model for every church setting in every culture throughout history. What we have in the early church is a limited description of a very unorganized, organic, passionate, messy, and exciting new movement with no specific description for how church structure or leadership levels were to be established. From this I certainly don't find biblical justification, based on church structure or supposed ministry offices, to restrict women from church leadership or using any of the gifts of the Spirit.

Another indication the Spirit gives gifts of leadership to women is found in Ephesians 4:8-12. In 4:8 we read:

This is why it says: "When he ascended on high, he took many captives and gave gifts to his people."

The Greek word used here for people is *anthropos* which means human. This word specifically refers to both men and women. The text then describes how people are given gifts as apostles, prophets, evangelist, pastors, and teachers (4:11). If these gifts were only to be given to men, a different word would have been used. We also need to remember the wisdom in I Corinthians 12: One gift cannot say to another, **"I don't need you."**

Gordon Fee speaks to this in Chapter 21 of *Discovering Biblical Equality: Complementarity without Hierarchy:*

Nowhere does the Scripture explicitly say, for example, that only men may hold certain church offices – especially since the idea of "offices" (as having priority and needing to be "filled" by someone) does not appear at all in the New Testament.

REFLECTIONS FROM CHURCH HISTORY

In much of church history, people called for women to be restricted from leadership in the church. This was most often based on a belief that women were in fact (ontologically) inferior to men. Here is a significant observation: The belief that restrictions are needed has not changed but the reasons for the restrictions have changed. Today, advocates of the restrictive/complementarian position contend because women are different from men, they complement each other and are designed for different roles. These roles are defined within a structure (hierarchy) where men are in a stronger position of power than women. Women need to be inclined to trust men as they willingly submit to their leadership. This justification for restricting women is a newer perspective developed in the past fifty to seventy-five years, especially in the world of American evangelical Christianity.

I believe this newer justification for restricting women has developed in part from real life experience. Over the past hundred-plus years as women have worked to gain and then received more opportunities in society, as well as in some places in the church, they have clearly demonstrated they are every bit as intelligent, capable, and talented as men. (It is also important to note, more progress in gender equality is still needed in our society today.) Experience has shown the flaws in the previously held justification for restricting women based on their inferiority. But, in light of this experience, instead of removing restrictions on women in the church some have constructed a new justification for restrictions.

Historically, this misguided view of women as weaker/inferior was the prevailing perspective in many societies, including the United States. Unfortunately, the church often conformed to the world in the way women were viewed and treated. However, in church history there also were many times and places where this patriarchal perspective was rejected, and women were honored in the Body of Christ while being actively engaged in the leadership of the church (including the New Testament). Beth Allison Barr offers an excellent overview of how women serving in leadership has been a historical reality in the church in many areas, including within the evangelical movement in America in the 1800s in *The Making of Biblical Womanhood: How the Subjugation of Women Became Gospel Truth*.

Our record on this is mixed but the church has often been a constructive voice and influence for gender equality. Church history shows us how the church often treated women with greater dignity than was common within highly patriarchal societies.

For some helpful reading on this issue from the perspective of church history, I have appreciated the writing of William Witt, professor at Trinity School for Ministry. He has several helpful articles on this subject under the category of "Women's Ordination" on his website at www.willgwitt.org.

8

PRACTICAL REFLECTIONS AND CONSIDERATIONS

L et's think about some of the important implications and consequences related to living with either the "restrictive" or "non-restrictive" position. As we do this, we will see again why this is such an important issue which impacts individuals, families, churches and their communities.

Here are six words that can help us explore the practical realities of this issue: *Confusion, Pain, Ministry, Power, Experience, and Reality.*

Practical Reflection and Consideration #1: Confusion

One of my struggles with the restrictive approach to women in leadership in the church is that it inevitably creates plenty of confusion. Here are some ways this happens:

> *Confusion flows because the core restrictive/complementarian position is simply illogical.*

Evangelical complementarians claim men and women are equal in being but unequal in role/function. They contend restrictions placed on women in the church aren't based on competency but rather on the need to follow a divine plan in which men offer leadership, provision, and protection and women are called to be inclined towards submission as they receive male leadership. They contend this is a beautiful vision that honors and benefits women.

Problems and confusion emerge when we realize the issue is not really about roles, the issue is one of power and authority, with men being affirmed as the gender to rule over women perpetually and cross-culturally. In this framework, roles are defined not by what one does but simply by being in a hierarchy of male authority.

To tell a woman, "In your being you are equal with men," but follow that by saying, "Your essential role is to live under male authority," is inconsistent and self-contradictory. This is like saying 2+2=5. Regardless of how some people try to construct this, the "equal in being but different in roles" comes off as confusing and inconsistent. This is not about roles; this is about women being placed in a subservient place due to one thing and one thing only: their gender, which is part of their very being. From Janet George in her book, *Still Side by Side: A Concise Explanation of Biblical Gender Equality:*

It is illogical to say a woman, no matter her ability, must be under the authority of men in every situation and, at the same time, say she is equally valued.

Rebecca Merrill Groothuis speaks to the problematic and confusing logic of the male leadership/restrictive position in Chapter 18 of *Discovering Biblical Equality: Complementarity without Hierarchy:*

So while woman is said to be equal in her essential being, she is deemed subordinate precisely because of her essential being. Yet the notion that woman is equal in her being yet unequal by virtue of her being is incoherent.

Patriarchalists consign women to a permanently inferior status in a hierarchy of spiritual authority, calling, responsibility and privilege, all the while insisting that women are not spiritually inferior to men but that women and men stand on equal ground before God. This position is logically incoherent and so cannot be true. Women do not stand on equal ground before God if God has permanently denied them spiritual opportunities and privileges to which every man has access.

Confusion flows because the line of restriction is confusing and arbitrary.

As soon as we say women should be restricted from certain opportunities for leadership in the church, it immediately becomes confusing as to what women can or cannot do. The restriction line is drawn in very random and arbitrary ways and confusion flows. Maybe this should tell us something. Here are some examples of where churches have tried to draw lines of restriction for women.

- Women can't speak at all (complete silence).

- Women can speak but not if men are present or in the room.
- Women can speak but not teach.
- Women can teach but only up to fourth grade, eighth grade, or maybe through high school.
- Women can or can't pray with men present.
- Women can't speak, pray, or read Scripture in worship, but they can sing a solo or play piano.
- Women can lead the worship service but can't preach.
- Women cannot lead a congregation in worship.
- Women can pray or teach during the mid-week service but not on Sunday services.
- A woman could be affirmed as a schoolteacher or college professor but not be allowed to teach boys or men in her church.
- Women can't be pastors at all, or, in some cases, they can be an associate, youth, or worship pastor but not a lead pastor.
- Women can serve on some or even most church boards or committees but not on the primary leadership or elder board/group.
- Women can be church members but are not permitted to vote in church decisions.
- A woman can teach in a university or seminary but not teach or preach in the church.
- A woman can chair or lead some church ministry teams or committees but not others.

These examples illustrate the confusion that flows from the restrictive position. In some cases, it leads to behavior that can be described as beyond confusing and into the realm of bizarre. For example:

- In one church, a female missionary stood next to a man and told him softly what she wanted to say and then he spoke the words for the congregation to hear so the audience would not hear the woman's voice.
- Men in one church didn't believe they should listen to a woman speak, but they wanted to hear a woman who served as a missionary, so they all went downstairs and listened through audio feed from upstairs to downstairs.

I heard one female pastor share that at one point her church asked her to teach during a Wednesday evening service but prohibited her from teaching in the Sunday morning service. In reflecting on this, she said, "I know I Timothy 2 can be a confusing passage, but I am pretty sure Paul was not saying women can teach on Wednesdays but not on Sundays."

In Chapter 1 of *How I Changed My Mind about Women in Leadership: Compelling Stories from Prominent Evangelicals*, John Armstrong offers this helpful perspective:

If I pushed these points logically, which I finally did, I found that every single church and complementarian leader I knew, had a different working list for what women could or could not do in the local church ... I finally had to ask myself: If this position that hinders women from certain ministry is so plain, why are there so many different positions that express it? ... If you are going to read these 3 "prohibitive" texts (I Corinthians

11:1-16, 14:33-35, and I Timothy 2:8-13) as opposing women in teaching and leadership, then why are they so difficult to actually understand and apply in our present context.

Confusion flows because of selective geographical and cultural application.

Confusion commonly results from the restrictive position because of the way it is applied in different places. For example, a church refuses to allow a woman to teach, preach, lead, or serve as a pastor in their church, while simultaneously supporting and affirming women who do those exact same things as missionaries in another society or setting. The message is: You can't do that here, but you can do it there.

This happens all the time, and it baffles me that people don't see this confusing inconsistency. Why is it okay to support a woman going overseas to preach and lead but it's not okay to do the same thing in their own setting and society? We also need to ask if some level of racism is present in these situations, but we're blind to it. Speaking of American churches, Gordon Fee says in Chapter 21 of *Discovering Biblical Equality: Complementarity without Hierarchy*:

Hypocritically (and with blatant racism) they "allowed" the woman missionary to teach the Bible to men in Africa or Asia but frequently forbade her to do so back home.

Confusion flows because of a confusing gap between the church and the world.

If one believes God has ordained women to fundamentally be in subordination to men and male leadership in the church, how about in other settings? For example, suppose you encounter a company, hospital, school, or a government group and you discover they have a policy that says: "In our group, we believe men, by virtue of their gender, are to be in leadership and authority over women. So, in our organization, men will always be the primary leaders. Women will not be eligible to apply for or work in certain positions of leadership. In our organization, there is a line of restriction for women that does not apply to men."

This might mean:

- A woman could be a nurse but not a head of a department or a doctor.
- A female schoolteacher could teach her class but not be an administrative leader or school principal.
- In a company, a woman could not lead a team or department. Or maybe they could lead some teams but not be a VP or CEO.
- Women working for a government agency would not be eligible to manage or lead a department.
- Women couldn't serve on the organization's board, or maybe they could be on the board but not be the board leader.

The list could go on and on, but you get this idea. This kind of mindset and practice is not as common in these settings today (thankfully), but I want to ask: If you are a Christian, how would your faith inform your response if you encountered this kind of situation in your school, company, or organization? If you are a follower of Jesus, how would you respond to an organization if they had this kind of policy and these types of restrictions on women?

Most people I know, Christian or not, would say this kind of policy is sexist, discriminatory, and deplorable. I certainly would. They would say it demeans women and is harmful to everyone in the organization. Many complementarians have told me they wouldn't support these kinds of restrictions, which clearly marginalize and oppress women, in their school or place of work. However, somehow, they are okay with not employing a woman as pastor, allowing women to preach, or to serve on a church leadership/elder board, or perhaps being excluded from serving as the chairperson of that board.

So, if I would condemn these kinds of restrictions based on gender as problematic in the marketplace, why would I want to celebrate and affirm the same behavior in the church? If I would condemn this restrictive behavior in a hospital, school, or company, how does it make sense to celebrate the identical restrictive behavior in the church? Again, confusing.

For myself, as a follower of Jesus who wants my life informed by the gospel and guided by my Lord in every area, I'd never support the types of restrictions I've described in any setting. Why? Because such behavior reflects a way of viewing and treating women that is deeply inconsistent with the biblical message and the implications of the gospel regarding our human identity, calling, and the life God longs for people to experience.

Here are some questions to consider as we reflect on the confusion that results from restricting women in their service in the church.

- If you oppose restrictions on positions women can hold in companies, schools, hospitals, and so on, why would you then say, "But come on into our church, we like to treat women that way here."?
- If you don't oppose these kinds of restrictions in the marketplace, what does that say about your view of women? Do you really think this reflects God's will for us?
- Some have said, "These kinds of restrictions in the workplace are indeed sexist and discriminatory but limiting women from serving as pastors or leaders in the church is different and isn't discrimination." When asked why, I've heard this response: "It's not discrimination because the Bible says it's okay." Hearing this I have three responses.

1. The Bible doesn't teach that. You have misunderstood the Bible.
2. Let's be honest. If this is discrimination in other settings, the identical behavior is also discrimination in the church; it's simply discrimination being justified in the name of biblical Christianity. (This is most unfortunate.)
3. To say it is different in the church because we are talking about "spiritual authority" is inconsistent and a confusing way of isolating the spiritual from the rest of the world.

This confusing gap between the church and the world also occurs when men find themselves working under the leadership of a female supervisor. If I were to hold the complementarian position with consistency and integrity, I would have to refuse to work for a female boss. But many Christian men who advocate for male leadership in the church simply ignore the implications of their theological position when they willingly work with a female supervisor.

Just to be clear, I'm fine with men working for a female supervisor. I spent three years working in business before I became a pastor and had a fantastic female manager. I am simply saying this is a dynamic that reveals inconsistencies and confusion for those who hold the restrictive position. It is confusing (hypocritical?) when Christian people condemn restrictive hiring practices and working opportunities based on gender outside the church while then affirming the identical restrictive practices inside the church. What I call this "weird gap between the church and the world" is extremely confusing. I cannot see the consistency of saying simultaneously:

- Restricting women from leading and using their gifts based on their gender is deplorable outside the church.
- In the church, I affirm, applaud, or even institutionalize these same restrictive practices.

Restricting women reflects a form of discrimination that is obvious to some but dismissed by others. This confusion should tell us something. Consider this statement from Greg Yee, pastor and conference superintendent in the Evangelical

Covenant church (*Covenant Companion Magazine* – September, 2019):

The same implicit bias that we talk about with race is applicable concerning women and leadership positions.

The non-restrictive position and practice of biblical equality leads to more clarity and less confusion.

Practical Reflection and Consideration #2: Pain

We need to be honest about the painful results of the restrictive position. Both men and women are hurt when women are restricted from using their gifts. Women are hurt, sometimes deeply, when they are called and gifted by the Holy Spirt to lead, preach, or teach and then told by their church family, "No, only men do that." This hurts men, too, as they miss opportunities to learn from women and experience the kind of community Jesus calls us into. This pain can be obvious as well as subtle.

I know my evangelical complementarian friends contend hurting people is not their intent or what their position causes. However, when women are prohibited because of their very being, their gender, from using the gifts the Holy Spirit has given them, the message sent and received is this: *You are less valuable, less capable, and less trustworthy than men.* There's simply no way to spin this differently. The restrictive position sends a message that is demeaning and disrespectful to women and the pain it causes is real.

Again, when looking at the passages in New Testament where spiritual gifts are described, there is never any mention of some gifts being given to men only or women only. Gifts are given as the Spirt chooses and not based on gender. To receive a gift from God but not be allowed to use it by the people of God is deeply damaging.

I have heard the stories, shared the tears, and seen the real pain of my sisters in Christ as they have wrestled with the reality of being marginalized in the very Body of Christ. I have seen the pain of men who are deeply hurt when they see their sisters treated in this way. The damage the restrictive position leads to in the church, home, and world is deep and real. We do well to acknowledge this and allow it to inform our ministry and life together in the Body of Christ.

The pain that results from creating a hierarchy of power that grants men power over women can run deep in so many ways. When men are granted perpetual power, it can lead to a spirit of entitlement and arrogance. It is harmful when women are forced to live at home or in a church culture where their faith will be questioned if they feel called to resist male authority. There is evidence pointing to the way the restrictive position that celebrates a hierarchy of male authority can lead to oppression and abuse in both the church and home. If you want to explore this, here are two articles you can find on the Christians for Biblical Equality website (https://www.cbeinternational.org/).

"When Religion Hurts: How Complementarian Churches Harm Women" May 19, 2021

"What are the Consequences of Theological Patriarchy" – May 26, 2021

While this is disturbing, it should not be surprising. How we think influences how we act and live. When we develop ideas and beliefs that portray women as less valuable, capable, and trustworthy than men, this inevitably will lead to women being treated as less than men. It's surprising that some refuse to acknowledge this reality. In Chapter 8 of *The Making of Biblical Womanhood: How the Subjugation of Women Became Gospel Truth*, Beth Allison Barr says with bold honesty:

Hierarchy gives birth to patriarchy, and patriarchy gives birth to the abuse of both sex and power. ... The historical reality is that social systems that invest some people with power over the lives of other people result in the destruction of people.

In Chapter 12 of *How I Changed My Mind about Women in Leadership: Compelling Stories from Prominent Evangelicals*, Alice Matthews offers this challenging message:

Satan wins a great victory every time the gifts God gave women are put on the shelf simply because the bearers are female. Considered in that light, the proscription of women from leadership in the church is not merely inconvenient; it is a sin.

The non-restrictive position and practice of biblical equality leads to more health and less pain.

Practical Reflection and Consideration #3: Ministry

When women are sidelined from the fullest opportunity to use their gifts, the ministry of the church suffers. We need to have maximum, not partial, participation in moving the mission of God forward. Let's not keep people on the sidelines.

A common response to this rather obvious observation says there are so many needs and opportunities for ministry any woman can certainly find ways to serve the Lord without needing to serve as pastors, preachers, or key leaders in the church. This response misses the point and honestly, it is superficial and patronizing. When everyone is invited to serve in whatever areas they are called and gifted, ministry will multiply.

There are times when someone wants or needs to be ministered to by a pastor they can trust as a spiritual mentor and leader. There are, of course, many people who can serve in this way who are not ordained pastors. However, sometimes a person will want or need the assistance of a "pastor" who has more significant theological training and the church's affirmation of ordination. In my thirty-plus years as a pastor, I have had countless experiences like this when someone has reached out to me for prayer, confession, mentoring, guidance, or pastoral care because I am a "pastor."

If gifted women are prohibited from serving as pastors, we minimize and dilute our ministry. At times, a woman will receive ministry most effectively from another woman, just as there are times when a man will need another man in his life for pastoral ministry. When there are no women pastors, we significantly and even tragically compromise our ability to have the most effective discipleship and pastoral care among the women in our church. Men also miss out on the potential blessings of having a female pastor as there are times when men need a female voice in their lives. Recognizing and valuing the need for both male and female pastors (both associate and lead pastors) and leaders is actually part of what it means to really value gender complementarity.

In Chapter 16 of *How I Changed My Mind about Women in Leadership: Compelling Stories from Prominent Evangelicals*, Carol and James Plueddemann say this:

I do respect hierarchical complementarian men and women who sincerely want to obey the Scripture. But as I look at a world in pain, a lukewarm church, and billions of people around the world who don't know Christ, I am passionate about the urgent need to employ the giftedness of the whole church. We shoot ourselves in the foot when we unbiblically limit the leadership gifts of at least half the Body of Christ. For the sake of the gospel, every gift is needed and no treasure can afford to be buried.

In Chapter 17 of *How I Changed My Mind about Women in Leadership: Compelling Stories from Prominent Evangelicals*, Minette Drumwright-Pratt shares this perspective:

I must add that on the mission fields, I witnessed God using women missionaries to lead both men and women in profoundly meaningful ways. With so much work to be done, God surely wants to use the abilities of every Christ follower.

The non-restrictive position and practice of biblical equality leads to more and better ministry.

Practical Reflection and Consideration #4: Power

Let's think about these words of Jesus from Luke 4:18-19 as he began his public ministry in Nazareth:

"The Spirit of the Lord is on me,

  because he has anointed me

  to proclaim good news to the poor.

He has sent me to proclaim freedom for the prisoners

 and recovery of sight for the blind,

to set the oppressed free,

to proclaim the year of the Lord's favor."

We see here the heart of Jesus for the hurting, the marginalized, and the oppressed. Caring for others who are marginalized and oppressed is one of the characteristics of a healthy, biblically functioning church. With this in mind, we need to give very serious consideration to this reality: Establishing a hierarchy in the church of male authority and power is deeply problematic and marginalizes women in the church. I know some will try to soften or justify this leadership/power structure in the church by saying it is all about roles and having men and women complement each other. I respectfully and strongly disagree.

Here is a strong statement, but I believe it is true: when women are prohibited from leadership and told part of their core calling and identity is to submit to male leadership/authority this places them in subjugation to men. This involves treating women in a demeaning and disrespectful way that compromises the biblical and gospel message. I fully agree with church historian Beth Allison Barr who says this in Chapter 7 of *The Making of Biblical Womanhood: How the Subjugation of Women Became Gospel Truth*:

The greatest trick the devil ever pulled was convincing Christians that oppression is godly. That God ordained some people, simply because of their sex or skin color (or both), as belonging under the power of other people. That women's subordination is central to the gospel of Christ.

Consider this sobering quote from Elaine Storkey in the introduction of *Scars Across Humanity: Understanding and Overcoming Violence Against Women:*

As the statistics calmly tell us, acts of violence to women ages between 15 and 44 across the globe produce more deaths, disability, and mutilation than cancer, malaria, and traffic accidents combined. The truth is that violence on such a scale could not exist were it not structured in some way into the very fabric of societies and cultures themselves. It could not continue if it were not somehow supported by deep assumptions about the value of women, or some justification of the use of power.

Our world is filled with so much social stratification as various groups strive to impose power and authority over one another. We in the church need to declare and display how Jesus wants to free us from the tragedy and sin of power abuse, sexism, and discrimination. This goes beyond issues of equality and justice to the biblically beautiful vision for unity among people. The world needs to hear and see a gospel driven message that offers a different view of power. The world needs to hear and see a gospel driven vision for human identity and relationships that transforms lives and communities. (Galatians 3:28, Colossians 3:11, Ephesians 2:11-22, Mark 9:33-35, Luke 22:24-27, John 13:1-17)

When we hold the restrictive position, we rob ourselves of the opportunity to share the gospel in the fullness of its beauty and goodness. We need to declare the way Jesus and his completed work on the cross frees us from the tragedy of patriarchy and frees us for a beautiful vision where men and women live and serve in unity. We need to see how Jesus and his gospel call us to live in all our relationships with mutual respect, love, and humility.

The non-restrictive position and practice of biblical equality leads to greater humility and unity and less oppression and power abuse.

Practical Reflection and Consideration #5: Experience

I want to acknowledge I am influenced by my experience. In more than thirty years as a pastor, I have always worked in churches where women and men served together on our church's primary leadership team or board. Having both men and women present has been invaluable. We have been better because we served together as brothers and sisters, serving side by side in the mission of Jesus. I am grateful for opportunities to serve in churches that have affirmed women in their calling and service as pastors, leaders, and missionaries.

I have served alongside amazing women of character and faith. I have learned from them when they preached. I have been blessed by them when they were my leader. I have watched them lead people to Christ, touch the hurting with compassion, lead and preach in a way that inspires people, and seen them assist people towards greater levels of spiritual maturity.

It breaks my heart to know there are churches and people who don't want these gifted and dedicated women using their gifts and serving their Lord in these ways. What a loss. I cannot begin to fathom how much poorer I and the church would be if these women had been restricted from serving fully into their calling with all of the gifts God has blessed them with.

The non-restrictive position and practice of biblical equality is something I have seen and experienced as beautiful and good.

Practical Reflection and Consideration #6: Reality

Let's be honest, throughout history and around the world today, there is a long and tragic story of women being treated terribly. Far too often, women are demeaned, dismissed, objectified, marginalized, oppressed, and abused. Consider these sobering realities.

- A woman is beaten every nine seconds in the U.S.
- Approximately one-third of women globally have suffered from violent abuse.
- One in five women in the U.S. have been raped in their lifetime.
- Every day, three women are murdered by a current or former spouse or partner.
- Some estimate that more than 20 percent of girls are sexually abused by the time they are 18 years old.

Sources: UN Women (unwomen.org), NCADV (National Coalition against domestic violence), the World Health Organization (WHO), The Center for Family Justice (CFJ)

If you want a sobering experience, do an online search for "Statistics for Women's Abuse." In addition, women are still often paid less for doing the same work as men. In some parts of the world, women cannot vote, drive, or have access to education.

These realities are heartbreaking. We need to ask:

- Where is the voice of the church of Jesus Christ? What is our message to a world where women are often viewed so poorly and treated with such contempt?
- Is our best response one that says women are supposed to live within a hierarchy of male power and authority?
- How has the position and practice that celebrates a hierarchy of male authority in the home and restricts women in their service in the church contributed to the presence of these hardships women experience and endure?
- Is the church better off when women are sidelined and their voice is removed from the leadership of the church? What does that say about how we view women? What are the consequences of treating women in such a demeaning and disrespectful way?

Kevin Giles offers a challenging and sobering perspective on the way theological patriarchy contributes to domestic abuse in his book, *The Headship of Men and the Abuse of Women: Are They Related In Any Way?* In the introduction, he writes:

Headship teaching can encourage, and legitimate domestic abuse and it must be abandoned if domestic abuse is to be effectively countered in our churches.

People with complementarian convictions of course condemn domestic abuse and claim their position does not contribute to this tragedy. They say their teaching on headship in marriage is good for women and children. The reality is a growing amount of evidence tells another story. If you resist this, I invite you to read Giles' book with an open mind.

Violence against women is a massive and tragic reality in our world. Elaine Storkey offers an extensively researched, challenging and honest look at this global crisis in her book *Scars Across Humanity: Understanding and Overcoming Violence Against Women*. She exposes patriarchy for the damage it does as she walks her readers through both gruesome statistics and heartbreaking stories.

If you read the paragraph above and think violence against women is not really a big problem and should not be viewed as a "crisis," I ask, challenge, implore you to read Storkey's book. She exposes the realities of early enforced child marriages, female genital mutilation, selective abortion and infanticide, honor killings and femicide, domestic violence, sex trafficking, prostitution, rape, and sexual violence in war.

This is a horrific list, and you might wonder, what does this have to do with women in leadership in the church or male headship in marriage? I contend they are linked in a very real way. I understand people who advocate for the restrictive/complementarian position sincerely condemn violence against women. However, we need to remember, our beliefs influence our actions. When the church advocates for the restrictive/complementarian position, regardless of how passionately it is presented and benevolent it is deemed to be, we contribute to the disturbing reality of violence against women. We become supporters of a form of theological patriarchy that can create a sense of entitlement among men that distorts their vision of women and their use of power. When women have unequal status in any context, they are far more vulnerable to any number of abusive actions from the men in power around them. As Storkey says in Chapter 11 of her book:

Patriarchy provides the basic building blocks on which the great edifice of violence against women can be built.

The non-restrictive position and practice of biblical equality leads to more dignity and respect for women and less disrespect and abuse of women.

Practical Reflections and Considerations: Concluding Thoughts

All these practical considerations are real. When women are told they are not eligible to serve in leadership in the same way as men the message sent is: *You are not as capable, valuable, or trustworthy as men.* I know people who embrace the complementarian/restrictive view will insist this is not what they are saying. However, I maintain this is exactly what they're saying; they just cannot see it or admit it.

The restrictive message results in inevitable confusion, more pain, and less ministry. It tragically contributes to the way women are mistreated in multiple ways inside and outside the church. When women are restricted from service in the Body of Christ, everyone suffers. People's service in the church should be based on giftedness, calling, and character. It should not be based on gender.

9

FINAL CONSIDERATIONS

S ome final thoughts for your consideration.

Being Conformed by the Word – Not by the World

Ironically, I have found some people will question the non-restrictive position by saying they want to go back to the Bible and be conformed by the Word (Bible), not by the world. They mistakenly believe this position is driven by secular society and values.

I agree; let's be shaped and guided by the Word of God and not by the world. YES to that! But let's remember that for two thousand years, the church too often and in too many places has been conforming to a patriarchal world more than being guided by the Word on this issue. In doing so, we compromised our gospel and biblical calling.

The position and practice of biblical equality does not reflect being driven by an extreme form of secular feminism or being conformed to the world in a problematic way. Actually, the church needs to stop conforming to a world that has so often had a flawed view of women, resulting in too much suffering and pain for far too long. Now is the time to get this right and be conformed by the Word. In Chapter 20 of *Discovering Biblical Equality: Complementarity without Hierarchy*, Roger Nicole states:

The great problem for Christianity is not that biblical egalitarians have been carried away by their desire to emulate secular feminism. Rather, the problem appears to be that the Bible-believing people have permitted themselves to fall below biblical standards because they were unduly influenced by surrounding societies in which the oppression (of women) prevailed in spite of centuries of Christian witness.

When in Doubt

I love Pastor Stuart Briscoe's story in Chapter 4 of *How I Changed My Mind about Women in Leadership: Compelling Stories from Prominent Evangelicals*. After extensive Bible study, he concluded that this is a tough issue. As he wrestled with this, he had a powerful encounter with God and the Scriptures when studying the parable of the talents (Matthew 25:14-30). He says:

Then one day I read again the parable of the man who before going away gave his servants gifts and promised on his return to hear an account of their stewardship. He was less than pleased by the one who misunderstood his master and buried his gift. I took to heart yet again the compelling truth that gifts are not imparted to be buried. But then like a thunderclap the thought occurred to me: What does the master think of those who bury the gifts of others? And I knew then that I, as a husband, father, and pastor, could do precisely that with the gifts of thousands of women. There and then I asked the Lord, "Whatever else You can accuse me of, please deliver me from being guilty of burying the gifts of those over whom I legitimately exercise some degree of spiritual oversight." And that was the tipping point for me.

I resonate with Pastor Briscoe as he describes the tensions he felt in his study, prayer, and service. Part of what moves me toward the position and practice of biblical equality is my desire to avoid burying anyone's talents. If you find yourself unsure how to understand this issue, I invite you to join Pastor Briscoe and lean into the position that will create more ministry and avoid burying the God-given gifts of our sisters in Christ.

Are Complementarians less Complementarian than Egalitarians?

I think so, and here's why. I fully agree with my complementarian friends that, while sharing the same essential humanity, men and women are also different. There is something very real, powerful, mysterious, and wonderful about being a woman or man that is unique to being female or male. Women and men have a shared humanity and identity as children of God, but we are not identical. Indeed, we can complement each other. So ...

- When it is time to assemble a leadership/elder team at a church, why would we want to eliminate the presence and voice of women? If women have something unique and valuable to offer specifically because they are women, as complementarians accurately affirm, why close the door on their presence? Excluding females implies we don't need them or what they have to offer as women.

- In a multi-staff church, when it's time to work together as pastors, why would we want to be sure no women have a place at this table? If women have something to offer that only they can, why restrict women from the circle of your pastoral team? How can we complement each other if we eliminate the presence of women?
- When it's time to learn from someone who can preach or teach, why would we want to hear only from men? Why assume we don't ever need to hear from a woman?

There is a contradiction going on when, with our words, we say to women: "We value you, need you, and you have unique things to offer," and then our actions say: "We do not want or need you in our leadership circle, we do not want or need you on our pastoral team, or we do not want or need to hear from your preaching."

Because men and women are different and can complement each other, I want both men and women serving and leading together in all areas of ministry in the church. I honestly believe I'm more complementarian than those who use this term as a way of describing why they restrict women from areas of leadership in the church. I believe in gender complementarity without hierarchy.

Says Howard Marshall in Chapter 11 of *How I Changed My Mind about Women in Leadership: Compelling Stories from Prominent Evangelicals:*

Further, it has become clear to me that the term complementarian is inappropriate since upholders of this view are able to produce lists of what women may not do in church but which can and must be done in a complementary fashion by men, whereas there is no corresponding list of what men may not do in church but which can and must be done by women. The complementary notion, in other words, is one-sided and inappropriate.

Biblical Interpretation: A Case Study from Luke 13:10-17

Let me highlight one more time these key thoughts before we take a look at a fascinating scene from the life of Jesus in the gospel of Luke.

- The position of biblical equality that supports women in leadership in the church comes from the Bible, not from a desire to conform to various movements in our culture.
- The issue of women in leadership in the church is an issue of biblical interpretation – not an issue of who believes in the authority and inspiration of the Bible with greater conviction.
- Bible study and interpretation is hard work – and well worth the effort. Am I approaching the Scriptures with a humble heart and teachable spirit, aware of my own tradition but not reading the Bible through my tradition?

- What did women in the Bible do with the clear calling, gifting, and blessing of God? What does the answer to this question tell us?

Let's take a look at an encounter Jesus had with a synagogue leader. Keep in mind this person was surely deeply devoted to the Scriptures and confident in his biblical knowledge.

¹⁰ On a Sabbath Jesus was teaching in one of the synagogues, ¹¹ and a woman was there who had been crippled by a spirit for eighteen years. She was bent over and could not straighten up at all. ¹² When Jesus saw her, he called her forward and said to her, "Woman, you are set free from your infirmity." ¹³ Then he put his hands on her, and immediately she straightened up and praised God.

¹⁴ Indignant because Jesus had healed on the Sabbath, the synagogue leader said to the people, "There are six days for work. So come and be healed on those days, not on the Sabbath."

¹⁵ The Lord answered him, "You hypocrites! Doesn't each of you on the Sabbath untie your ox or donkey from the stall and lead it out to give it water? ¹⁶ Then should not this woman, a daughter of Abraham, whom Satan has kept bound for eighteen long years, be set free on the Sabbath day from what bound her?"

¹⁷ When he said this, all his opponents were humiliated, but the people were delighted with all the wonderful things he was doing. (Luke 13:10-17)

This religious leader responded with what he thought was a crystal-clear understanding of the Scriptures. He knew what it said, but Jesus reveals he didn't understand what it meant and how the Scriptures should be applied.

How did this person miss what was so clear to Jesus?

- He isolated the Sabbath law from the rest of Scripture. He was so focused on that one portion of Scripture he didn't allow the rest of Scripture to help him discern how to understand and apply the Sabbath law.
- When Jesus demonstrated divine power, this religious leader missed what God was doing. He could not get past his narrow focus on this one portion of the law.
- As a religious leader who saw Jesus gaining influence, could it be that his fears and struggle with the potential loss of power was actually the driver here, impacting his understanding of Scripture and his response to this situation?
- He tried to make a literal and simplistic application of this law when the situation did not call for it.
- He was oblivious to how he was already ignoring the Sabbath law himself. This reflects a lack of self-awareness and likely a dynamic where he had been doing certain things a certain way for so long (leading his ox to water on the Sabbath) that he struggled with reflecting on his own position objectively.
- With a clearly supernatural miracle right in front of him, he was blind to what was happening. This

religious leader was suffering from a hard heart, a
lack of self-awareness, and a closed mind.

This passage should challenge us to not miss what God may
be doing right in front of us. I think about this when I reflect
on the many times I have seen God use women in beautiful
ways as they have served Him as lead pastors, associate
pastors, and church leaders.

Jessica Carter has written a helpful book called *Troubling
Her: A Biblical Defense of Women in Ministry.* In Chapter 1,
she explores the meaning of this scene in Luke 13 and offers
these challenging and insightful thoughts.

*For the synagogue leader, the entire situation was governed by
the Sabbath laws, the command was so clear. So far as he could
tell, he was right. Except he was wrong.*

*Sure he quoted the verse correctly, but he did not understand
what it meant in relation to the rest of the Scriptures. He
couldn't make sense of the Sabbath, Jesus, the miracle and the
woman, so he relied on one set of verses. Even worse, he thought
he had a zeal for God, but he was actually fighting against
God's Son.*

*This is very similar to what is happening in Christian circles
where women in ministry is opposed. God is using women all
over the world to preach the gospel and to minister to His
church. The gifts and calling of these women are evident. But
in the face of all of this evidence, their leaders continue holding
on to a verse or two that they don't understand. And they do
this, despite having a clear example of their behavior set forth
in Scripture.*

What Do I Love About My Church?

Here is another way to think about this: If you are a Christian, imagine a friend asking you, "What do you love about your church?" Which response would you want to give?

First, from the *restrictive* perspective:

"You know, I just love the way our church restricts women from being leaders. In our church, I love our commitment to limit the voice and influence of women. In our church, women can't be pastors and we don't allow them to preach in our worship services. I think this is a good way to treat women and it makes us a healthier community."

This may seem like hyperbole, but this is what the restrictive position says and where it lands. So, we need to ask, "Is this is something I would love about my church?"

Or second, from the *non-restrictive* perspective:

"You know, our world is filled with relational heartaches and the tragedy of racism, sexism, and class discrimination. I love the way our church strives to live into a different vision for relational life which Jesus gave us. I'm grateful that we don't have any restrictions on women around the ways they can serve or lead. I know some churches restrict women, but we believe the Bible teaches us that women are called and gifted by God to serve and lead in the church just like men."

As a pastor, I have often enjoyed the opportunity to respond to this question. Yes, the church has problems, but I really believe there are so many things to love about the church. However, I have a hard time understanding how one would be excited to share how the restrictive perspective is something to love about the church. I honestly struggle with seeing how the restrictive position is good news for anyone.

A Concluding Overview of this Subject

Discovering Biblical Equality: Complementarity without Hierarchy, edited by Ronald W. Pierce, Rebecca Merrill Groothuis, and Gordon D. Fee, is one of the best and most thorough resources for understanding the position of biblical equality. I want to share this quote from the book's introduction. This offers a great summary of what is at stake as we live into the life and mission Jesus has for us.

If you hold to my teaching, you are really my disciples. Then you will know the truth, and the truth will set you free (John 8: 31-32). So promised Jesus Christ, the Lord of the church and the cosmos. The cause of Christ is advanced only as truth is recognized, affirmed and lived out with wisdom and integrity. Truth must be brought to the world as well as to the church. Doctrine that falls short of the truth not only impedes believers from walking in the full freedom of the gospel of grace and truth but also hinders unbelievers from coming to salvation through the work of Jesus Christ.

This book is born of the conviction that both the world and the church urgently need to hear and take to heart the message of biblical equality, because it is at once true, logical, biblical and beneficial. The essential message of biblical equality is simple and straightforward: Gender, in and of itself, neither privileges nor curtails one's ability to be used to advance the kingdom or to glorify God in any dimension of ministry, mission, society or family. The differences between men and women do not justify granting men unique and perpetual prerogatives of leadership and authority not shared by women. Biblical equality, therefore, denies that there is any created or otherwise God-ordained hierarchy based solely on gender. Egalitarianism recognizes patterns of authority in the family, church and society—it is not anarchistic—but rejects the notion that any office, ministry or opportunity should be denied anyone on the grounds of gender alone. This is because women and men are made equally in God's image and likeness (Gen 1: 27), are equally fallen (Rom 3: 23), equally redeemable through Christ's life, death and resurrection (Jn 3: 16), equally participants in the new-covenant community (Gal 3: 28), equally heirs of God in Christ (1 Pet 3: 7), and equally able to be filled and empowered by the Holy Spirit for life and ministry (Acts 2: 17).

Consequently, any limits placed on the gifts and abilities of women should be challenged through a rigorous investigation of the biblical texts—rightly interpreted and harmonized with the whole of God's Word. Biblical egalitarianism (as opposed to any brand of secular or pagan feminism) is biblically based and kingdom focused. It does not rest its arguments on secular political movements or a theologically liberal denial of the Scripture's full and objective truth and authority for all time. Moreover, biblical egalitarians apply the basic historical-grammatical method of interpretation and the best principles of theologizing to their task. They make no appeal to "women's consciousness" as normative; neither do they feel free to dispense with or underplay any aspect of sacred Scripture, since it is all equally God-breathed and profitable for all of life (2 Tim 3:15-17). Biblical equality, while concerned about the false limits and stereotypes that have fettered women, is not "woman centered" but God-centered and concerned with the biblical liberation of both women and men for the cause of Christ in our day and beyond. For when women are denied their gifts and callings, men suffer from the omission as well.

This book is part of an ongoing controversy among evangelical Christians over the meaning of gender, ministry and marriage. Though varying expressions of an exclusive male leadership have persisted in the church and home over the last two millennia, a remnant has always been present to speak on behalf of biblical equality between men and women. This voice became stronger and clearer after the Reformation, especially at the turn of the nineteenth and twentieth centuries, and during recent decades has been expressed by a host of evangelicals who hold firmly to the inspiration and authority of Scripture. This volume is built on the faithful work of those who have preceded us.

10

TWENTY QUESTIONS

These questions are intended to challenge the assumptions of the restrictive position and help us wrestle with the implications and realities of this position.

1. If there is a list of things women cannot do because of their gender, where is the list for men?

2. What has been and is the cost of restricting women from serving in all areas of the church? What has resulted for people and churches living with this restrictive position?

- How many people have been hurt?
- How many ministry opportunities have been missed?
- How much abuse has been unknowingly encouraged?

3. What specifically is it that makes a woman unfit for leadership? Just her gender? If so, is she really being viewed as equal in being?

4. Is the position that restricts women about "roles" or is it about power and control?

5. In what ways and for how long has the church conformed to a world where so often and in so many places forms of patriarchal sexism have prevailed? Historically, has the church too often conformed to the world, rather than the message of Jesus and the Bible, in the way we view and treat women?

6. Do I believe God is at work in the world, at work beyond the walls and obvious sphere of the church? When voices outside the church begin to affirm biblical values like gender equality, why not celebrate this? Are there times when Spirit-led movements in the world are aligned with God's will, even if some voices in the church miss this?

7. Given the way God used Deborah to lead the nation of Israel, why would I think God would never want to use a woman to preach a sermon or pastor a church?

8. Where in the Bible do we find a clear prescriptive teaching on church organization or leadership offices?

9. Women speak in the Bible with instruction and inspiration (i.e.: Miriam, Deborah, Hannah, and Mary). So, how can the voice of women be heard in the Scriptures themselves but not in the church?

10. Since Junia was identified as an apostle (Romans 16), on what basis are women restricted from leadership?

11. Throughout history and around the globe today, there have been and are numerous cultural settings that can be described as patriarchal, where men have had or have more power and privilege than women. We are talking about hundreds of times and places where this dynamic has existed. In these settings, women have been and are restricted in ways that don't apply to men. Given this, can even one society be identified with such a patriarchal social system where it's clearly produced positive benefits for women? Can we identify even one historical or contemporary example of a patriarchal society in which women flourish because of this environment? Is there even one example that shows women treated with an increasingly abundant level of honor and respect in such a setting? Even one?

12. How sobering is it that from Genesis to Revelation, the biblical text that most specifically describes a relational hierarchy of male authority over women (Genesis 3) describes this not as a beautiful or good thing but as a tragic result of sin which leads to great hardship?

13. When a person, pastor, or church prohibits a woman from following God's calling and using her gifts, is this a perspective that needs to change or a sin that needs to be confessed ... or both?

14. If I insist the church be a place that restricts women, would I also support the same kind of restrictions outside the church? If I do support placing restrictions on women in all settings, what does that say about my view of women? How do I justify that kind of overt discrimination? If I don't support gender discrimination in the marketplace, why would I support it in the church?

15. Do I have a blind spot on this issue?

16. Consider again Galatians 3:28: **There is neither Jew nor Gentile, neither slave nor free, nor is there male and female, for you are all one in Christ Jesus**

Why is it that many Christians point to this verse as a wonderful and inspiring word to guide us away from racial and class discrimination but somehow ignore what this says about gender discrimination? What would you think of a church that restricted people from leadership based on their ethnicity or class? If you object to such discrimination, why would you support gender discrimination?

17. If I believe women should not serve as pastors or preach in an American church, am I okay with a female missionary pastoring or preaching in another country? If so, does this make sense?

18. If you like movies, I think you'll love this one. "Hidden Figures" raises questions about racial and sexual discrimination in this story about female African American mathematicians working at NASA during the Space Race. I invite you to watch it, enjoy it and then ask yourself: Do I really want to view and treat women the way many of the women in this film were viewed and treated? Would I want this type of dynamic in my church? Is this the way of Jesus? The racial and sexual discrimination these women experienced was tragic. Is it really any different in the church when women are prohibited from serving in certain positions of leadership because of their gender?

19. Fifty years from now, how will we look back on the ways some Christians promoted the idea and practice that men are

entitled to a position of power, privilege, and authority over women? How will we reflect on the ways women were prohibited from certain opportunities to serve and lead in the name of biblical Christianity? Will we look back on this with the same guilt, confusion, embarrassment, and regret that we have when we reflect on the efforts of many Christians who years ago justified slavery in the name of biblical truth?

20. God trusted women to be the first to declare the most important message the world had ever heard – He is not here! He is Risen! (Matthew 28). So why would we want to restrict or limit their voice today? Remember, women have been preaching the resurrection since Mary Magdalene and the other Mary in 33AD! (Matthew 28)

11

THE MOST IMPORTANT QUESTIONS

As we conclude, I want to thank you for reading and engaging with this issue and invite you to now consider what I think are the most important questions.

Who is Jesus Christ?
How will I respond to him?

I ask you to consider these two questions with the following thoughts in mind.

Jesus Christ is unique, even incomparable. As the divine son of God, Jesus is the author and giver of life. Jesus conquered death when he rose again to new life after his death on the cross. Jesus can give you an identity and a purpose that can transform your life. Jesus offers forgiveness, hope, wisdom, and strength. Jesus offers you the most authentic and powerful freedom you will ever find. Jesus also calls you to live beyond yourself as you participate in his mission and movement in the world.

Following Jesus does not mean you will have a problem-free life with a guaranteed pathway to comfort and prosperity. However, Jesus is the one who can lead you in profound ways today and into an eternal destiny with him in heaven. You are invited into a life-changing relationship with Jesus Christ today as you follow him in a personal way.

Ultimately, the biggest question is not *What does the Bible teach us about women in leadership?* The biggest questions are *Who is Jesus Christ* and *How will I respond to his invitation to follow him as the Lord of my life?* Responding to these questions involves asking *Did Jesus rise from the dead* and *Is his offer of salvation real?* C. S. Lewis reminds us in a concise and brilliant way what is at stake:

Christianity, if false, is of no importance, and if true, is of infinite importance. The only thing it cannot be is moderately important.

If you choose to follow Jesus, you will need to accept this reality: There are millions of Christians and thousands of churches, and some will hold beliefs and engage in practices you don't support. But that doesn't change what is at stake as you decide to live with or without Jesus.

I know people who resist becoming a follower of Jesus because they are confused and offended by the way some churches practice a restrictive approach towards women in leadership in the church. Some are offended by the position that advocates for marriage as a union centered in male authority and female submission. If this frustrates you, please know this is not the story of every church or every follower of Jesus. Do not let confusion or frustration over this issue keep you from following Jesus or being faithfully engaged in church life. Honestly, if you struggle with the ways some churches restrict women and define marriage around a hierarchy of male authority, I believe your instincts and desire for something better actually comes from God.

If you want to consider these two most important questions and explore the message of Jesus in a fresh way, I recommend any of these books.

- *Mere Christianity* by C. S. Lewis
- *Simply Christian* by N. T. Wright
- *Making Sense of God* by Tim Keller
- *Who is this Man* by John Ortberg
- *In the Grip of Grace* by Max Lucado

12

WHY I GRIEVE AND WHY I HOPE

M y concluding personal reflections.

I DO GRIEVE.

I grieve for the ways the church and Christian people have so often viewed and treated women as less valuable, capable, and trustworthy.

I grieve for the hurt this has caused within the very Body of Christ.

I grieve over the way the church's position and practices regarding women in leadership have compromised our message to a hurting world. We live in a world that desperately needs the gospel and the beautiful implications of the gospel. Our world needs a gospel-driven understanding of power, people, service, and humility. Our world longs for and needs to see the way the gospel breaks down the hierarchal social systems based on class, gender, and ethnicity. Social systems structured to marginalize people have plagued societies throughout history. I grieve the ways the church has often diluted the beauty and power of the gospel message by restricting and marginalizing women while placing them in a hierarchy of male authority.

I grieve the ministry opportunities that have been lost. I grieve our inability in the church to offer the best possible pastoral care and discipleship for women when they could benefit from the service of a female pastor. And I grieve the opportunities many men have lost because they've not had a female pastor who could have spoken uniquely into their lives from her place as a woman.

I grieve for any and all ways various forms of theological patriarchy have contributed to the extensive and tragic marginalization and oppression of women in the church, home, and throughout the world.

I grieve for the women who are deeply devoted to Christ and who are clearly called and gifted for leadership but are told to stay on the sidelines.

I DO GRIEVE, BUT I HAVE HOPE!

I hope and pray for a day when the Body of Christ can function better and shine brighter as men and women increasingly live in unity and serve side by side. I long for the day when there is an unanimous consensus in the church of Jesus Christ that gender equality is a biblical value to support and celebrate. I have hope as I see many women serving so well as pastors, missionaries, preachers, and leaders in the church. I have hope as I see men and women advocating for the biblical vision of biblical equality and complementarity without hierarchy.

I draw hope from the lessons of history and how God sometimes moves and brings about change over many years. We see this throughout church history and certainly as we reflect on the reformation movement in Europe in the 1500s. We see this when we look back on the church in America in the 1700s and 1800s. It took many years, but the church eventually moved from using the Bible to justify slavery to using the Bible to condemn slavery for the sin that it is. I have hope that one day the church will stop using the Bible to restrict women. Rather, may the Bible increasingly be used to invite women to serve fully with all the gifts they have been given in all areas of the church.

I have hope because the church gives me hope. I love the church. It is true; sometimes the church is an embarrassing and hypocritical mess. But the church can also be a community of life, faith, hope, and love where people are transformed in beautiful ways and communities are blessed. The church has been moving forward around the globe for two thousand years, and I live with hope that this momentum will continue.

More than anything else, I have hope because Jesus gives me hope. I have hope because I believe Jesus wants women to serve him freely and fully. Ultimately, I have hope because I believe Jesus will get His church where he wants it to be. I have hope that women will be affirmed in their gifts and callings as pastors, preachers, prophets, teachers, and leaders because I believe this is what Jesus is hoping for.

May God bless his church and use his church to bring blessings to a broken and hurting world. May God increasingly bless his church with women and men serving in unity as sisters and brothers in Christ. May we move forward in humble trust as we live in the hope that only Jesus Christ can provide.

No longer will there be any curse (Revelation 22:3)

Now to him who is able to do immeasurably more than all we ask or imagine, by his power that is at work within us, to him be glory in the church and in Christ Jesus throughout all generations, for ever and ever! Amen! (Ephesians 3:20-21)

May the God of hope fill you with all joy and peace as your trust in him, so that you may overflow with hope by the power of the Holy Spirit. (Romans 15:13)

QUESTIONS FOR LEARNING TOGETHER

We often learn best in community. After reading this book, consider inviting friends to enjoy a "book club" type of gathering and conversation. Use this book as a resource for initiating thoughtful discussion with others. Outlined below are some questions to guide your discussion.

1. What or who has influenced your life in the area of women in leadership in the church? Have there been churches, authors, people, or experiences that shaped your perspective on this issue? Elaborate.

2. How important is the issue of women in leadership in the church to you? Why?

3. What are some of the principles you value when it comes to interpreting the Bible accurately?

4. What do you think are highlights from Genesis 1-3 that can help us understand God's vision for this world and how men and women can share life and ministry together?

5. Are there insights from the Old Testament that speak to you regarding the way women can lead as they serve God?

6. What can we learn from Jesus about how women are to be viewed and treated?

7. What can we learn from the New Testament church regarding women in leadership in the church?

8. How do you understand what I Timothy 2 and I Corinthians 11 & 14 teach us on this subject?

9. This book emphasizes six words (see Chapter 8) to be mindful of when considering the practical implications of our position on women in leadership in the church (Confusion, Pain, Ministry, Power, Experience, Reality). Do you have any specific responses to any of these words and the associated thoughts that are offered in this book?

10. What is your response to the idea that slavery can be a relevant and revealing parallel for us as we consider our position and practices related to women and leadership in the church?

11. Do you have any thoughts on any of the six "final considerations"?

- Being conformed by the Word or the world?
- When in Doubt ....
- Are complementarians actually less complementarian than egalitarians?

- Biblical Interpretation: A case study from Luke 13:10-17
- What do I love about my church?
- The summary comment from *Discovering Biblical Equality: Complementarity without Hierarchy*

12. Among the list of twenty questions in Chapter 10, are there one or two you find especially interesting, challenging, confusing, frustrating, encouraging, or enlightening? How so or why?

13. Are there specific highlights from this book that were especially helpful to you?

14. Are there any steps of application you feel called to take in response to reading this book?

15. Do you have any other thoughts, reflections, or questions that come from reading this book?

RECOMMENDED RESOURCES

I hope my book has been helpful to you on a subject of great importance.

Here are some other books I recommend.

- *How I Changed my Mind about Women in Leadership* (Alan Johnson Editor)
- *Discovering Biblical Equality: Complementarity without Hierarchy* (Edited by Ronal Pierce, Rebecca Groothuis, and Gordon Fee)
- *Rediscovering the Scriptures Vision for Women: Fresh Perspectives on disputed Texts* by Lucy Peppiatt
- *How to Read the Bible for all its Worth* by Gordon Fee and Doug Stuart
- *The Blue Parakeet* by Scot McKnight
- *Junia is Not Alone* by Scot McKnight
- *Troubling Her: A Biblical Defense of Women in Ministry* by Jessica Carter

- *The Making of Biblical Womanhood: How the Subjugation of Women Became Gospel Truth* by Beth Barr
- *Still Side by Side* by Janet George
- *A Week in the Life of a Greco-Roman Woman* by Holly Beers
- *The Silent Queen: Why the Church Needs Women to Find Their Voice* by Paul Ellis

If you enjoy learning with videos, search on YouTube for resources from N. T. Wright on "women in ministry."

Fuller Seminary (Pasadena, CA) has an excellent article written by the late David Scholer on their web site (fuller.edu) that offers a helpful summary of the biblical message on this subject. "Women in Ministry: A Biblical Basis for Equal partnership".

Christians for Biblical Equality (CBE) has numerous articles and resources on their website. You can find them at cbeinternational.org.

CBE exists to promote the biblical message that God calls women and men of all cultures, races, and classes to share authority equally in service and leadership in the home, church, and world. CBE's mission is to eliminate the power imbalance between men and women resulting from theological patriarchy.

ABOUT THE AUTHOR

John Jenks has served as a pastor with the Evangelical Covenant Church for more than thirty years. He also has served on staff with Mount Hermon Christian Camp and Conference Center in Northern California. He graduated from UCLA (BA/History) and Fuller Theological Seminary (MDIV).

John and his wife Ann live in Santa Barbara, California, where he currently serves as a campus chaplain with Covenant Living at the Samarkand.

John is available as a guest speaker, seminar leader, and consultant for churches exploring the issue of women in leadership in the church. Contact him at johnwjenks@gmail.com.

WORKS CITED

Barclay, William. *Commentary on John*.

Barr, Beth Allison. *The Making of Biblical Womanhood: How the Subjugation of Women Became Gospel Truth*. Brazos Press, 2021.

Bartholomew, Craig, G., and Thomas, Heath A. *Manifesto for Theological Interpretation*. Baker Academic, 2016.

Beck, James R., Gundry, Stanley, N., and Belleville, Linda L. *Two Views on Women in Ministry*. Zondervan Academic, 2005.

Carter, Jessica Faye. *Troubling Her: A Biblical Defense of Women in Ministry*. Purple Girl. 2010.

CBE International. "What are the Consequences of Theological Patriarchy." Christians for Biblical Equality, May 26, 2021. https://www.cbeinternational.org/resource/article/

mutuality-blog-magazine/what-are-consequences-
theological-patriarchy

Evangelical Covenant Church. "The Biblical & Theological Basis for Women in Ministry," https://covchurch.org/wp-content/uploads/sites/2/2011/02/2-Women-in-Ministry.pdf

Fee, Gordon D., and Stuart, Douglas. *How to Read the Bible for All Its Worth,* 4th edition. Zondervan Academic, 2014.

George, Janet. *Still Side by Side: A Concise Explanation of Biblical Gender Equality,* Revised Edition. Christians for Biblical Equality, 2019.

Giles, Kevin. *The Headship of Men and the Abuse of Women: Are They Related In Any Way?* Cascade Books, 2020.

Johnson, Alan F. *How I Changed My Mind about Women in Leadership: Compelling Stories from Prominent Evangelicals.* Zondervan Academic, 2010.

Keller, Timothy. *The Reason for God: Belief in an Age of Skepticism.* Penguin Books, 2008.

McKnight, Scot. *Junia Is Not Alone.* Patheos Press, 2011.

Morgante, Camden. "When Religion Hurts: How Complementarian Churches Harm Women." Christians for Biblical Equality, May 19, 2021. https://www.cbeinternational.org/resource/article/mutuality-blog-magazine/when-religion-hurts-how-complementarian-churches-harm

Ortberg, John (Pastor). Willow Creek Church Leadership seminar.

Peppiatt, Lucy. *Rediscovering Scripture's Vision for Women: Fresh Perspectives on Disputed Texts.* IVP Academic, 2019.

Pierce, Ronald W., Groothuis, Rebecca Merrill, and Fee, Gordon D. *Discovering Biblical Equality: Complementarity without Hierarchy,* 2nd edition. IVP Academic, 2005.

Peters, Marianne. "Called by God." *Covenant Companion Magazine;* September 2019,

Plantinga, Cornelius. *Engaging God's World: A Christian Vision of Faith, Learning, and Living.* Eerdmans, 2002.

Scholer, David. *Covenant Companion Magazine*; 1984.

Snodgrass, Klyne. "A Case for the Unrestricted Ministry of Women." *The Covenant Quarterly*, May 2009.

Snodgrass, Klyne. Covenant Church Theological Symposium (2018).

Snodgrass, Klyne. *Ephesians (The NIV Application Commentary Book 10).* Zondervan Academic, 2009.

Storkey, Elaine. *Scars Across Humanity: Understanding and Overcoming Violence Against Women.* IVP Academic, 2018.

Walter, Gary (Pastor). *Covenant Companion Magazine*; June 2016).

Wenrich, John (Pastor). *Covenant Companion Magazine*; September 2019).

Will, William. "Women's Ordination. www.willgwitt.org.

Yee, Greg, (Pastor). *Covenant Companion Magazine*; September 2019).

Made in the USA
Middletown, DE
22 August 2022

71159281R00106